CACHUCHA

FANNY ELSSLER

FANNY ELSSLER
IN AMERICA

A cut-out of the lost American lithograph after Henry
Inman's portrait of Fanny Elssler in her dressing-room at the
Park Theatre, painted from life. The print was drawn on
stone by Henry Ph. Heidemans and published by Endicott
in 1840. The well-known Kohler print done in Munich
five years later is a smaller version of the American print,
altogether weaker, and in reverse.

IN

-⁜-

COMPRISING SEVEN FACSIMILIES OF RARE AMERICANA—NEVER BEFORE

OFFERED THE PUBLIC—DEPICTING HER ASTOUNDING CONQUEST OF AMERICA

IN 1840-42: a *Memoir*, a *Libretto*, two *Verses*, a *Penny-Terrible Blast*,

Letters and Journal, and an early *Comic Strip*—The Sad Tale

of her Impresario's Courtship.

-⁜-

WITH AN INTRODUCTION AND NOTES BY ALLISON DELARUE.
The souvenirs and illustrations, unless
otherwise credited, are from his collection.

-⁜-

DANCE HORIZONS, NEW YORK: 1 9 7 6

International Standard Book Number 0-87127-084-6

Library of Congress Catalog Card Number 75-37381

Printed in the United States of America

Dance Horizons, 1801 East 26th Street
Brooklyn, New York 11229

FRONT COVER:
A contemporary cut-out of Fanny Elssler in *La Cracovienne*
is incorporated in the binding design.

ENDPAPER ILLUSTRATION:
Double brass plaque, possibly used for embossing.
Elssler is shown on the Left in *La Cachucha* and on the right
in *La Cracovienne*. From the Harvard Theatre
Collection, Gift of Allison Delarue.

Table of

CONTENTS

List of

ILLUSTRATIONS

Henry Wikoff, Paris, 1836.

Historical Background to

AMERICA'S ELSSLERMANIA

By Allison Delarue.

HISTORICAL BACKGROUND TO AMERICA'S ELSSLERMANIA

In the summer of 1839, Stephen Price, a partner in the management of the Park Theatre in New York, looking for a means to retrieve the fortunes of the house, decided to engage Fanny Elssler. It was an ambitious decision as no dancer of Elssler's caliber had yet appeared in America. From her native Vienna, Elssler had gone on to be crowned in Naples, Berlin, London and, finally, Paris—the ultimate goal of a dedicated dancer. Price did not know the dancer personally and sought the assistance of his friend Henry Wikoff, a gentleman from Philadelphia living in Paris. Wikoff, long interested in the theatre, was an Elssler fan and had followed her triumphs in London and Paris. Fortunately, he knew the Marquis de La Valette, Elssler's protector, and through him he made the dancer's acquaintance.

Fanny Elssler was intrigued by the offer, although hesitant; the intense rivalry between her and Marie Taglioni at the Paris Opéra had come to an impasse and it was expedient to look for other worlds to conquer. Henry Wikoff introduced Elssler to some of his influential friends in the American colony in Paris which made her realize that Americans were not the barbarians the French had led her to expect. While it had not been easy to induce the ladies of the American colony to receive an opera dancer, the gentlemen were delighted to meet her and they promised to supply letters of introduction to prominent friends in the States. Consequently, Fanny Elssler signed the contract, but not without trepidation.

Soon after this decision was made, Stephen Price

Letter from Fanny Elssler to Henry Wikoff.
From the Princeton University Collection, Gift of Allison Delarue.

died and his partner, Edward Simpson, decided not to honor the contract, much to Elssler's embarrassment since the press had already announced the engagement. After the failure of other negotiations, Henry Wikoff came to Elssler's rescue, turned impresario and assumed full responsibility for her tour of America. He had Victorian qualms about the "freak" of having his good name connected with that of an opera dancer, but, as far as Wikoff could see, Fanny Elssler's behavior was lady-like and surprisingly modest.

Henry Wikoff at once made full use of Elssler's accumulated legends and launched advance publicity in the *New York Morning Herald* through his friendship with its editor, James Gordon Bennett. No luxury import ever had more fashionable puffs in the press. Elssler arrived on the steamer Great Western accompanied by her impresario; her ballet partner and ballet-master, James Sylvain; her cousin and companion, Katti Prinster; and her coachman, Charles Neal. She made her debut at the Park Theatre on the evening of May 17, 1840. It was gala: the bon ton were out in full force. The theatrical furor was unique. Theatre managers booked Elssler for other cities up and down the East Coast, undaunted by Wikoff's fee of $500 a performance. Lithographers quickly ran off easel-print and music-title portraits of Elssler in her various roles. She sat in her dressing room at the Park Theatre for Henry Inman, the leading portrait painter of the day. The reviews in the press rivaled the verse inspired by the dancer.

Fanny Elssler had a six-month leave from the Paris Opéra. However, she broke her contract and continued to tour the States, with appearances in Havana, over a period of two years, giving a total of

Interior of the Park Theatre.

Woodcut from *The New York Polyanthos.*
From The New York Public Library Collection.

208 performances. The tour was a conquest: according to a saying in the theatre, "It was not Columbus who discovered America; it was Fanny Elssler."

But Fanny's bouquets were not all sweet. Wikoff's publicity had been successful in presenting her to the American public as a fashionable import, but it had taken all of his personal contacts to convince ladies that an opera dancer was not a show for men only. For a year Fanny Elssler went in royal progress from one city to another. Elsslermania was unchallenged. But, in the summer of 1841, rumors of scandal burst into print. Evangelical piety was rampant at the time and an opera dancer inspired no less pious humbug than the denizens of the red-light district. Horace Greeley began an anti-Elssler campaign in *The Tribune*. He attacked the "harlot Fanny" who, he said, had not "the common excuse of necessity for a life of wantonness and shame." George Washington Dixon, the editor of a lurid sheet, *The New York Polyanthos*, jumped into the act with Goreyish stories, amusingly illustrated with cartoons. Because of Elssler's high fee, Dixon accused her of taking bread from the mouths of babes. After Wikoff took Fanny for a rest to a fashionable hotel in Coney Island, *The Polyanthos* ran the headline: "The Great Kicker Kicked Out." Main Line Philadelphia guests at the hotel had made a scene over the fact that Wikoff's suite adjoined Elssler's, although the press at the time referred to her as "Madame Wikoff." Far from being kicked out, Fanny Elssler packed up in "high dudgeon," shook the sand from her slippers, and declared that watering place a provincial bore.

"A Lady of This City," who published a spurious life of Fanny Elssler at this time, may well have been a staff member of *The Tribune* or *The Polyanthos*.

The writer's work is garbled and fictitious. Fanny was said to be the daughter of a wealthy Viennese merchant who suffered losses and sacrificed his daughter as an opera dancer, fully aware that the stage was a jumping-off place to prostitution. The fictitious father turned out to be a poor sport: Elssler's success saved his business, but the subsequent seductions caused him to "curse and disown" her for bringing dishonor on the family name. A penny terrible! The Napoleonic legend had served Elssler as publicity at her Paris debut—but it was a legend. She was never set up in a villa as the mistress of the Duke of Reichstadt. It is unlikely that they ever met. Equally fictitious was the author's account of an affair with the Duc d'Orléans in Paris.

The anti-Elssler campaign was a dismal failure: the Park Theater was sold out nightly. Philip Hone wrote in his diary that he continued to follow Elssler's performances, as many others did, to protest the "insufferable arrogance, undertaken to write down this amusement, and abuse those who go to see it, calling them fools and idiots, and lying abominably about proofs of admiration bestowed upon this graceful *danseuse*. This sort of interference between men and their consciences, and dictation as to matters of taste, has become very common of late, and people seem determined not to submit to it." At no time during the anti-Elssler campaign was Fanny's reputation as a dancer questioned.

For the correct facts of the dancer's life and a full account of her American tour, the reader is referred to Ivor Guest's definitive biography: *Fanny Elssler* (Adam and Charles Black, London, 1970).

Fanny Elssler was the greatest dancer of the Romantic Ballet to cross the Atlantic and one of the treasures in our dance heritage. It is hoped the memorabilia offered here will help to recapture some of the excitement of that period. For our Bicentennial, let us take as our motto Fanny Elssler's last words on the American stage at her final curtain call at the Park Theatre, New York, on July 1, 1842: "Let me conjure you to be faithful to what you have so nobly begun."

—A. D.

The author extends his special thanks to Jeanne T. Newlin, Curator of the Harvard Theatre Collection, for granting the loan of La Tarentule *and* Memoir of Fanny Elssler, *and to the Boston Public Library for granting permission to use* A Short and correct sketch of the Life of Mad'lle. Fanny Elssler. *All of the other souvenirs, unless otherwise credited, are from the author's collection.*

MAD.^{lle} FANNY ELLSLER.

IN THE GRAND BALLET

LA GITANA

Fanny Elssler in *La Gitana*.

Fanny Elssler's exit at Coney Island. *The New York Polyanthos.*
From The New York Public Library Collection.

Fanny Elssler in *The New Smolenska*.

Memoir of

FANNY
ELSSLER

MEMOIR OF FANNY ELSSLER*

During Elssler's tour Henry Wikoff kept the *New York Morning Herald* informed of every move. At her second New York engagement, in August, Wikoff wrote James Gordon Bennett, the editor of the *Herald*, that he contemplated a "grand article" on Fanny. The first installment appeared in the *Herald* on the fourteenth: "We do not remember," Wikoff begins the article, "ever to have seen anything in the shape of a memoir of this divine *danseuse*. We shall, therefore, attempt a faint sketch of her career, as an accompaniment to the above representation of her in *La Cachucha*. It is somewhere about twenty-two years since, that the charming Fanny first came into this breathing world." This was in 1840, and Fanny Elssler was born in 1810. The *Memoir*, which appeared anonymously as a pamphlet, was publicity.

*Harvard Theatre Collection. Gift of the author.

MEMOIR

OF

FANNY ELSSLER:

WITH ANECDOTES OF HER

PUBLIC

AND

PRIVATE LIFE!

FROM HER CHILDHOOD TO THE PRESENT TIME.

Her step so light—her brow so fair,
She boundeth like a thing of air ;—
Or fairy in her wanton play,—
Or naiad on the moonlit spray.
Like gossamer on wings of light,
She floats before our tranced sight.
Let's gaze no more—nor speak—nor stir—
Lest we fall down and worship her.
Ford's Benighted Travellers.

NEW YORK:
PUBLISHED BY TURNER & FISHER, 52 CHATHAM STREET,
AND
15 NORTH SIXTH STREET, PHILADELPHIA.
1840.

PREFACE.

In inditing a memoir of a performer on whom all the superlative panegyric of our language has been lavished, it is difficult
to select terms of sober commendation which will not appear tame,
and even insipid. The newspaper press has so teemed with
eulogium—has so ransacked vocabularies for hyperbolical expressions,—that plain words have lost their force, and a plain man
incurs the charge of want of taste, who delivers his sentiments in
the language of reason and nature. Foreigners have made this
exaggerated mode of expression, ground of grave charge against
the American press. When confined to the Nimrod Wildfires,
and Roaring Ralph Stackpoles of the West, it is merely amusing,—
when it mingles with our literature, it is as so much dross to the
metal,—and when it pervades our ephemeral publications, every
enlightened conductor of a periodical sheet must regret that a
severer taste does not prevail.

Fulsome encomium usually defeats its aim. The performer
of real merit is injured by bald puffery. The man of sense
despises it, and even the inexperienced are not long misled by it;
—and should the public discover that they have given too much
credit to an actor's abilities,—the re-action under-rates his talents
in a more unjust degree, than his former elevation was unde-
served. Players have been sometimes destroyed by an over-
weaning desire on the part of their friends to exalt them in
public opinion beyond their deserts, and perhaps no performer
who has ever visited our shores could have sustained uninjured
the torrent of ranting rhapsody elicited by the perfections of
Madamoiselle Elssler,—except the subject of our memoir herself

It would be well if some literary Father Mathew should arise amongst us, teaching us temperance in our sayings,—as that reverend reformer urges temperance in our doings.

We all know that one of the canons of good breeding commands us to be surprised at nothing. Some years ago we visited Niagara in company with a cockney Chesterfield. He had never seen the Falls,—and descending the "Biddle Stairway," we were suddenly near the foot of the Cataract. We turned to mark the mute awe of his countenance. He had raised his *lorgnette* to his eye, and exclaimed "There's a considerable splash, isn't there?"

We are not sure however that in the few brief pages that follow, we shall be able to practice the virtue we preach:—and it would be still worse, if, in the effort to suppress our enthusiasm, we should descend to dulness. May our theme preserve us from this,—for he who fails when Elssler is the subject of his story, should never wield goose quill again:—he should go, and sin no more,

"And deeper far than ever plummet sounded,
Should drown his"—pen.

MEMOIR OF FANNY ELSSLER,

THIS most extraordinary woman was born in Vienna, in Germany, in the year 1818, of respectable parents, who had no connexion with the opera; —she being the first of her line who ever entered public life. Every one must hope however that the pursuit of the stage by her family may not end in her own person—but that she may be " the mother of a race of "—dancers,—all as excellent and graceful as their gentle mother.

One of those slight and trivial chances on whose pivot the most momentous events turn, placed our heroine in the Imperial Academy of Vienna. A Coryphean of the opera dwelt in a house adjoining the residence of Herr Elssler. An intimacy had subsisted between the families, and the glitter of the dancer's stage dresses had often dazzled the vision of the admiring sisters, Fanny and Theresa Elssler, and they begged their friend with the earnestness of childish eloquence to procure them admission to the theatre that they might see those gorgeous robes exhibited on the stage. Their father,—a prudent man, who had other views in life for his daughters—long witheld his consent; but moved by the entreaties of the lovely little suppliants, he, at length consented that they should visit the opera—*but once.* Alas! how vain is human foresight,—how futile human caution! That "once," determined the destiny of the good old man's cherished offspring. His slow consent wrung from him by a childish whim, gave the world such an artist as perhaps the world never saw,—and will send his name—now levying tribute of admiration from all civilized nations—down the stream of time—filling the memory of old men like a halo—as they recount—a fireside legend—to the marvelling children of another generation the wondrous exploits of "La Belle Elssler."

As the night of the Prince's Ball changed the fortunes of Cinderella,—so as we have hinted, the first night at the Opera implanted in the breasts of these young girls, a passion which fixed their lot in life. Their senses were entranced by the performance, and the impression then made on our heroine has never been erased. To prove that the poetry of motion is not the only sort of poetry she possesses, and that the sacred fire pervades her mind, as well as inspires her feet, we will translate here *literally* an expression which fell from her lips, when speaking of her feelings on her first visit to the Opera. We think a sublimer thought never entered the mind of man. "When I went in, and the light fell over me, I thought the place was heaven, *illuminated in honor of God's victory over Satan!*"

'Twould be tedious to follow the tyro through her studies. She was a winged Psyche on the night Taglioni made her debut in Vienna, and her young ambition burned to emulate that queen of the Graces. Her progress was so rapid that contrary to settled custom, she was not placed in the Corps de Ballet; and when the Directeur assigned her a station in the Corps Coryphean, she begged with modest confidence that she might be entrusted with a principal part in the Ballet. The Directeur was surprised, that a child—for she was then only twelve—should make such a request; but remembering her precocity, answered that he would try her powers. A short time elapsed and to her surprise, delight and terror, she found herself called on to rehearse the principal part in the beautiful ballet of "La Fee." We Americans cannot well understand the position in which our youthful heroine was now placed. The Ballet on the continent of Europe, and that to which the same name is given on the continent of America, bear about the same resemblance to each other as Fanny Elssler's dancing does to that of Mr. James Crow Rice. The production of a new ballet in Europe, is an event that follows months of incessant preparation;—outlays, of which we have no conception here,—practice, drilling, and exercise among the corps, the severity of which would exhaust a military martinet. The distribution of the characters is a duty assumed by the critics instead of the manager;—the progress of the rehearsal is watched by the public with an anxiety that would surprise us phlegmatic Yankees—the *training* and *condition* of the heroine are attended to, like those of a race horse,—and when, at last the momentuos night arrives, the people go to the theatre, as to some solemn festival. Hope or fear pervades every bosom; spectators, as well as actors are in a state of nervous excitement. The immense crowds that throng Box, Pit, and Gallery, are speculating on the coming performance, when the ominous tap of the leader is heard through the house, and the confused hum subsides into the silence of the grave. The overture is begun—finished—and the applause perchance is long and loud. Observe that man standing in a box near the stage. His hair is long, or rather, tall, for each individual of the shock seems endued with the same rigidity that contracts his thin features, and points to every angle, from zenith to the horizon His brows are drawn down, and his eyes are bent on the Orchestre with an intensity painful to see. His nostril is dilated, because his violent suspiration is carried on through that organ alone. His lips are pressed so firmly together, that his sharply cut mouth looks like a mere line. He grasps the cushions of the box so tightly that the blood under his nails has been forced back, and left the fingers as hueless as his face. He is the Composer of the ballet. During the Overture just finished—that man has lived an age. Each bar of the music was an era in his life. Once or twice, either himself or the band had slightly lost time, and the throes of death seemed to be shaking him. You could not perceive by any motion of his body that he was noting the time, and in instrumentation so complex, 'twould be difficult to detect discord among so many skillful professors as those before us, without some sort of bodily demonstration—but the maestro *was beating time with his soul!*

If the Ballet succeed, all those principally concerned in it become famous,—if they were not famous before;—humble talent is elevated, and fortune, as it always should be, is the reward of merit.

Madamoiselle Elssler's success in " La Fee," was unequivocal, and her career thenceforward was rapid, and brilliant,—beyond precedent. She was scarcely fourteen when the Neapolitan royal family invited her to their Capital. We fear we shall be accused of falling into the error we denounced in the beginning of these pages when we say, that at Naples her career was one blaze of glory. The royal family delighted to honor her, and her smiles were courted by the noblest in the land. She returned to Vienna, and was immediately installed as Premier Danseuse of the Imperial Opera. Here it was that the only son of Napoleon became madly enamoured of her. The Duke de Reichstadt—king of Rome—whose birth was considered at the time, the most important event that had taken place in the world for many centuries, —was a young man whose mind and body were delicately constituted, and the fascinations of Madamoiselle Elssler took such entire possession of his faculties, that it was said his health suffered from the effect of his passion. Under these painful circumstances our heroine resolved to withdraw herself from Vienna. King Ferdinand had seen her dance at Vienna, and received her most graciously at Berlin. The old monarch is reported to have said in the theatre—" She brings back my youth to me."

New triumphs awaited her in Berlin. It now
began to be conceded on all hands that "La Belle
Elssler" was the first dancer in Germany—and the
Directeur, by order of the King, offered her a permanent engagement on any terms she should herself propose. As a further inducement for her to reside in Berlin, an annual life-pension of about $3000
was offered her under a condition that she should
dance there each season for eight years. This
fortunate young girl rejected these high offers, and
in 1834 she left Berlin for London. To follow
her from London to the Continent, and there from
city to city, would be only to record her triumphs
wherever she moved. She led captive the hearts
of all. Offers of marriage from men in the first
circles of society met her in every city. She was
followed from London to Paris by bevies of infatu-
ated swains,—and her traveling train at length
resembled a royal cortege. In many places the
enthusiasm of the populace was carried to absurd
and degrading excesses. It was a common occurrence for foolish young men to unharness her
horses and draw her carriage to her lodgings ;—
a practice which we blush to say has been imitated
in one instance in this country. The wildest enthusiasm furnishes no excuse for such base servil-
ity. Madamoiselle Elssler felt herself degraded by
such a despicable proceeding ; and, in Baltimore,
the next night, she sought her lodgings privately,
and on foot.

An anecdote is told of Elssler exemplyfying
her moral courage and genuine benevolence, which
should not be omitted even in so short a sketch as
this. She was one day walking alone in the streets

of Berlin, and the balmy softness of the evening
wooed her to extend her walk toward the northern
suburb of the city. On her way home she was
slowly passing a miserable looking house, when the
low sob of a female struck her ear. Ever sensi-
tively alive to the cry of distress, she stopped,
listening for a moment;—the groan was repeated
accompanied with the feeble wail of an infant.
Judging from the exterior of the building that
poverty was its inmate, she was now aware that
sorrow, and perhaps sickness also dwelt there.
Her heart swelled at the thought, and overcoming
her natural reserve, she knocked gently at the
door. A weak, but sweet voice bade her enter,
and stepping into the room she indistinctly beheld
a woman lying on what seemed but a bag of straw.
There was no other furniture in the wretched
place, excepting a stool which stood beside the bed.
The invalid,—for such she seemed—desired our
heroine to be seated, and encouraged by the kind
interest in her fate expressed by the latter, she related her tale of sorrow. 'Twas a common case;
—though less common in Germany than in our
own country. She had a husband whom intemper-
ance had transformed from a man to a brute. He
had once been a respectable artisan, but had sacrificed property, reputation, health, to the fearful
cravings of the Rum-Fiend. The infant of the
unhappy woman was a month old, yet want of
nourishment, added to the abuse of the monster
whom she called husband, had prevented her
leaving her bed. Until this moment Elssler had
scarcely known that misery existed in the world.
Here sat she,—the cherished child of fortune, who

had princes as suitors—for whom the whole earth seemed wreathed in smiles—on whom thousands gazed with rapture,—here she sat beside the lowly couch of squalid wretchedness,—listening to a recital of such bitter misery, as she had not deemed could form a necessary part of this beautiful world. But she sat not long. The texture of the eternal chain that binds man to his fellow man, had not become indurated in this young creature's bosom by contact with a cold world. The links were fresh as when they drew her to the fountain of her mother's breast,—and she sank on her knees beside the stricken daughter of sorrow,—while the tears of sympathy flowed fast and free,—the holiest tears that fall from human eyes—those shed for suffering mortality.

While Elssler yet knelt over the low bed of the invalid, the door was burst suddenly open, and a bloated ruffian staggered into the middle of the room. 'Twas the husband. Elssler retired to the verge of the room, and the increasing darkness, prevented the fellow's becoming aware of the presence of a stranger. He threw himself into the chair, and the frail implement was crushed beneath his realing weight. This accident was sufficient to stir up the demon in the drunkard's heart. He commanded his wife to rise, and procure him another seat. She meekly replied that there were no more chairs, and she was too weak to rise. The inhuman villain raised a broken fragment to strike her. Elssler, with one bound, sprung from the spot where she had been standing and stood before the monster like an accusing angel. Brutality and cowardice are inseparable qualities.   The superstitious dastard shrunk back aghast—and Elssler, taking advantage of his panic, assisted the terrified woman to rise,—and hurried her, with her infant in her arms, into the street ; then following herself, she held the door by the handle of the latch on the outside,—at the same time entreating the passers by to secure the wretch within,—who by this time, recovered from his stupor, was straining at the latch.   Several men rushed in and overpowered the ruffian, while others assisted the fainting woman into the nearest house.   Elssler placed in her hand a purse, and hastily informing her of her place of residence, and assuring her of future aid,—she bounded towards her home with the step of a startled fawn.

A few days after this adventure, a cortege consisting of most of the nobility of Berlin, was proceeding at a rapid pace out of the gates of the capital on their way to the Cassino of the Duc de R —, where a splendid féte was to be given in honor of our heroine—who was now, as usual, the cynosure of all eyes.   The attention of the gay troop was arrested by Elssler's having suddenly wheeled her palfrey to the road side, where sat the poor woman she had rescued a few evenings before.   Will it be believed ?—the unhappy wretch was begging alms—imploring the passengers in the most heart moving tones to enable her to purchase the release of her abandoned husband, whose ill-treatment of her, had consigned him to a prison.

O ! woman ! how pure—how deep—how holy is thy love !   All other emotions and passions of the human heart wither and die, when their causes change or fade,—but the love of woman draws its nurture from itself.   Those qualities in the object which called it into existence, may be, as they had never been,—or change into their most frightful opposites,—but her love changes not—ceases not, —it is immutable—eternal! it gushes from her heart in a living stream, free and pure as at its birth, nor feels it ebb, until that heart be broken!

The end of this little incident is—that the polluted earth has received the drunkard into her all-absorbing bosom, and his sorrowing widow is still a pensioner of Mademoiselle Elssler.

It is said that Elssler possesses the most adroit tact in evading,—rather than repelling,—the too pressing advances of her numerous admirers. The following little story is in point. The leading facts are so well known, that we fear the recital will be tedious to many—but as the details may be new to some of our readers, we give the anecdote as briefly as possible.

A Crowned Head found its royal heart captured by the captivating Fanny. Kings, it is well known, do not woo like their subjects, and the royal lover conceived that it was only necessary that his august wishes should be known, to be joyfully complied with. A courtier waited on Elssler, and stated as a matter of business that the King regarded her with an eye of favor. She replied, that she felt greatly flattered, and hoped to deserve the good opinion of his majesty. The nobleman informed her that the monarch would hold himself at leisure on the following Thursday, when the *artiste* might visit the palace and have a private interview with the sovereign. This amounted to a command, which it would be disastrous for her to disobey. She promised compliance, and the messenger departed. She then began to cast about for some means to avoid the interview, or include in it a third party. Her sister Therese entered at the moment, and it was agreed between them that the latter should visit the palace—making it appear a mistake ; and as the King had not expressed any preference for Therese—indeed had never seen her,—she felt no apprehensions as to consequences.

At the appointed hour therefore, the sister of our heroine presented herself at the palace and was instantly conducted into the presence of the sovereign. When all had withdrawn, he commanded her, though in a condescending tone to raise her veil ;—she complied, and instead of the lovely features of Fanny, he started to behold the less beautiful,—but still beautiful—countenance of Therese.

" How's this—how's this ?" said the King, " I sent for Elssler."

" I am Elssler, sire," modestly replied the girl.

"Yes—yes—I suppose so—but I didn't mean you," said he pettishly—" I want Elssler—*the* Elssler." "I beg your majesty to pardon the error"—said Theresa, retiring.—" Your majesty's commands shall be instantly obeyed."

"Stop,"—exclaimed the King—" not now, it has become too late. To-morrow,—same hour— do you hear ?—no more mistakes—remember— *the* Elssler."

Therese withdrew with a low courtesy.

"Fanny! Fanny!" exclaimed the lively girl when she reached home—" Your fate is only deferred. The king insists on seeing you to-morrow."

She then related the particulars of the interview.

"He wants *the* Elssler !" said Fanny, archly, "Why, Therese, he must surely mean our father. Run, and inform the old gentleman that the King commands his presence at the palace at four o'clock to-morrow. Tell him to send up his name —"*the* Elssler," remember—he will be instantly admitted." Away skipped the laughing girl, and Fanny sat down to invent new schemes to baffle her royal lover.

The king had laid aside his dignity and had arrayed his person in the most attractive gear his taste suggested, and was now pacing his study with impatient step. He was still smarting under a cutting sarcasm levelled at him by the queen, in rather a public manner, on his supposed infidelities, and now, like all other men, similarly circumstanced—for kings *do*, sometimes, act like other men—he was resolved as an act of justice to his august spouse, to endow her next matrimonial suspicion with a large admixture of truth. He was fortifying himself in his praiseworthy resolution when, 'the Elssler,' was announced.

"Admit her, and retire," said he. The sexual, appellation sounded oddly to the gentleman in waiting ; but as his duty was plain, he ushered the father of all the Elsslers into the presence of royalty.

"Who the devil are you?" said the monarch fiercely, and with the most unkingly selection of language.

This reception was colder, or rather warmer than the old gentleman expected,—and he replied, somewhat falteringly—"my name, your majesty, is Elssler."

"Elssler!" interrupted the king in a rage; —"More Elsslers!—In heaven's name, how many are there of you!"

"Why, your majesty,"—began the alarmed old man—"I have two brothers, Felix and Herman, besides—"The fiend seize your brothers," exclaimed the enraged monarch. "I wish they were at the bottom of the Rhine, and you holding them there. Ho! Jan! turn this idiot into the street!"

The old gentleman required little urging in his egress from the palace; and as he wended his way homeward, he fell into a deep cogitation on the event just passed. "What *could* his majesty," mused he, "have wanted with me? Therese distinctly told me the interview was to be private, and the business important; and yet he did'nt seem to know me, and when I told him my name, he started with disgust, as if he had tread upon a live rat. He wished my poor brothers at the bottom of the river too. Perhaps Herman and Felix have been plotting treason—I'll go and warn them of their danger."

Consternation spread through all the ramifications of the family—Elssler. Each member lived in hourly apprehension of arrest,—and their fears were not allayed when it was known to them that Fanny—the pride—the glory of their house, had been peremptorialy summoned to the palace.

Our heroine entered the royal presence with timid step, and downcast eye,—and when harshly commanded to remove her veil, the full blaze of her surpassing beauty, so softened the king, that he forgot his chagrin and took her hand with his most gracious smile. He led her to a seat, and said in his blandest manner, "The pleasure I feel in your society is enhanced by the difficulty I've had in procuring it."

"Difficulty, sire!" said Elssler, innocently. "Surely nothing can be difficult with your majesty, you have but to utter your royal commands, and myself—nay, the whole of the Elsslers will attend your majesty." The smile on the lip of Fanny, was so slight that the king failed to observe it, and replied :

"Why, yes, I've had some of them here already. But 'tis yourself,—your charming self whom I had delay in seeing—which delay I am anxious to repair, by at once soliciting a kiss from those beautiful lips." Fanny retreated back a step or two towards the door, when it was suddenly opened, and the Gentleman Usher announced "the Queen." His majesty started to his feet and exclaimed, "how dare you sir"—"her majesty insisted,"—deprecated the Usher, as the stately personage entered the room. She frowned darkly on seeing Elssler, who with ready tact knelt at her feet, and said in a tone of the utmost simplicity— "His majesty has sent for me to communicate the pleasing intelligence that he will graciously condescend to patronize my first benefit, which takes place on Monday next —and he has just told me that he had sent for you, madam, to meet me here, and said he had but little doubt but that you, most gracious madam, would also honour the theatre with your illustrious presence." There was an awkward pause.

Elssler had an acquaintance with several of the royal household, and she had obtained the promise of a gentleman Usher—at some hazard to himself,—to acquaint the queen that his Majesty required her presence in his study, at four o'clock, and thus our heroine so fearlessly repaired to the palace. But the gentleman had taken a sober second thought on the consequences of delivering a false message to the queen-consort,—and broke his promise. Meanwhile one of the female spies

of the jealous queen had informed her **Majesty**
that a veiled female had ascended the king's private
staircase on the previous afternoon. The same
vigilant emissary had given her Majesty information that the *same* young woman, had just entered the king's study. This had brought her most
jealous queenship to the scene of action. Now
here was a dead lock. The king looked marvellously like a loafer detected in the act of steal-
ing a watermelon;—her majesty's eyes shot forth
most illustrious fury;—and Elssler knelt,—con-
gratulating herself that her wit had prevented
a family quarrel, and at the same time rid her
of the importunities of the king. The queen was
the first to speak.

"Rise, young woman,"—said she with asperity,
—"you were here yesterday."

"I was not, madam," said Elssler rising with
dignity.

"Then why are you here at all?"

"At the command of my Sovereign, madam,
—with your majesty's permission I will withdraw."
"Stay," said the king—having now gathered up
the scattered fragments of his dignity, and taking
the hand of Fanny,—"Stay, young lady—I respect
your virtue no less than I admire your talents. I
now perceive why I have seen *two* of your name
before, and I assure you I cannot too often see the
third—*at the theatre*. Accept this ring as a token
of my esteem,—and I pledge my royal word, that
the King *and Queen*, will be in their Box, on the
night of your benefit—Farewell." He kept his
word, and he was her constant patron while she re-
mained in his dominions. His costly present may
be seen on her finger flashing through the theatre
on any night when she dances the *Pas El Jalio
de Jeres*.

Dr. Johnson says Shakspeare " exhausted worlds and then imagined new." Only the latter part of this line will apply to our heroine. Figuratively, she had not exhausted Europe, nor worn herself out there. On the contrary,—though she has indeed reaped one golden harvest, she has, like a skillful husbandman, allowed the soil to lie fallow for future cultivation. She *imagined* new worlds, and came to America to find them.

Elssler left Bristol in the Great Western, on the fifteenth day of April, and arrived in New York May third—having been eighteen days on the passage.

She entered New York without an engagement. She was, however, well assured of employment. She came to us in a most unpropitious season. The principal theatre in the country had long been labouring under the most distressing reverses—and in fact, theatrical affairs throughout the United States, were suffering under a languor, that threatened utter prostrastion. Elssler had fixed her terms at more than double the amount that has ever been paid to a performer in this country,— and the manager of the Park theatre engaged her with fear, if not with reluctance. She had brought letters of introduction to some of the oldest and best families in New York, and this together with her great European name, gave her an *eclat* which was sure to fill her first house. After much delay in drilling the meagre, awkward Corps de Ballet, she appeared on the Park boards on the 14th. of May, last, in the Cracovienne, and Tarentule. She describes her trepidation on this occasion, as greater than she ever before experienced. She had been told in Europe that the Yankees were a people who had no dancing in their souls, and that their appreciation of Terpsicorean excellence went not beyond the "breakdowns of Virginia."

The French papers warned her that she would receive no favor here: our notions they said were so prudish that anything like an abbreviated garment would be visited with national wrath;—and as in the Cracovienne, and some other dances,—her steps were thought sufficiently liberal even for the French Capital,—that here, aught approaching a free use of her limbs would be a signal for the horror-stricken burghers to leave the Theatre and pass an ordinance requiring her to quit the country, under penalty of fine and imprisonment. Under these impressions it is not wonderful that the heart of Elssler quailed when she heard the surging of the crowd,—the uproar of its getting seated, and the tumult with which an American audience always sinks into quiet. We shall never forget her first *appearance* on the boards. No man *saw* her enter. When the eye first rested on her, she was standing in the centre of the stage, like

> "The sculptured statue on the gate of Altorf,
> That looks life—yet neither breathes, nor stirs."

She went through the dance,—but her agitation told unfavorably on the performance. Towards the close however, it was evident she was getting confidence,—and her last *pas* was executed with a brilliancy that struck the spectators like the discharge of an electric battery. The Rubicon was passed—she was safe. She played in New York fourteen nights—and upwards of $20,000 were received during that period at the box-office; more than twice the amount that a single person ever drew to that house before.

On the seventeenth of June she appeared at the Chesnut Street Theatre, Philadelphia, and performed for eight nights, with a success wholly unprecedented in this city. On the eighth night she sprained a tendon of her foot, which detained her four days longer. She repaired to Washington, and the affairs of the nation were forgotten in the rush of legislators to the theatre. She returned to Baltimore, where the boxes were sold at auction—many commanding $3 for a single seat for one night.

At Baltimore she sustained a pecuniary loss, owing to the embarrassment of the Manager of the Theatre there. Her attraction had overflowed the treasury—yet at the end of her engagement the manager did not pay her, but offered his note for $1200. Elssler offered to relinquish her claim for $400 to enable the Manager to pay the Corp de Ballet, which he, notwithstanding, failed to do. She then offered to perform for their relief one night gratuitously. This they gratefully declined, alleging it is said the uncertainty of obtaining the money from the manager after it had been received. She then with untiring generosity paid all their expenses back to their respective homes.

Monsieur Sylvain—*en passant* the best male dancer ever seen in America—got nothing for his benefit, and sued the manager for the amount. Mr. Walton has published a statement of this transaction, accounting for the money—but whatever may be the opinion in Baltimore,—we fear he has failed to convince the public in other cities of the fairness of his dealings.

After this engagement she rested a short time from her severe and unusual labours—unusual because in Europe but one, or at most two performan-

ces are required of her in a week. On the Twelfth
of August she again commenced in New York
with unabated attraction. This was the more
surprising as two-thirds of the wealthy population
was, and still continue, absent from the city. It
was supposed that she would sail for Europe during
the present month, but her unexampled success in
this country induced her to solicit from the Directeur of the *Academie de la Musique* at Paris an
extension of her *furlough*. She will therefore
remain in the United States for the ensuing season,
visiting Boston, Philadelphia, Buffalo, Cincinatti,
Charleston, Natchez, Mobile and New Orleans,
where $10,000 have been offered her for six weeks
performance.

Before Elssler appeared on the Park boards, she attended the
Theatre, to witness the last appearance in America of Miss Jane
Shirreff, the popular vocalist, and it is believed the rumour that
the former would appear in the Boxes drew more to the house
than the talent of the fair beneficiare. On her third night
she received a flattering tribute from a kindred spirit, and
sponsorial namesake. Mrs. Fanny Kemble Butler repaired to
New York the moment she heard Elssler had appeared, and the
distinguished ex-tragedian threw the first boquet of the evening
at the feet of the *danseuse*.

It is with a feeling of deep regret that we in closing our pages,
are constrained to record an indirect outrage on our accomplished
heroine in New York. Our prescribed space will allow us only
to state that a number of German musicians had resolved to compliment their fair countrywoman with a splendid serenade, beneath the windows of her hotel. This was a delicate tribute to
her surpassing talent, and at the same time a grateful acknowledgment for her disinterested generosity in performing a night
in Philadelphia, gratuitously for one of their distressed countrymen. Rumour of this intended concert had become circulated,
and several thousand respectable citizens congregated near the
spot to enjoy the music. A gang of rioters enjoying the sobri-
quet of Soap-locks, Butt-enders, and Round-rimmers had assembled, and a man named Dixon, with several others, deliv-

24

ered inflammatory speeches in the Park. The burthen of these addresses was the injustice of patronising foreign, in preference to native, talent, and allusion was made to an unfortunate affray that occurred last winter in which a man named Armstrong—the former leader of this gang—was killed by some Germans in their own defence. The serenaders ignorant of the presence of foes, had erected their music stands and began the concert, when a descent was made on the unoffending minstrels. Many of their valuable instruments were broken, and themselves assaulted. One man received a severe stab in the neck. The Germans fled, and the assailants collected the shattered instruments, and burned them in the street. We have no room for comment—but the daily press has stamped this outrage with the infamy it deserves.

Elssler's visit to the United States has not benefited herself alone, even in a pecuniary sense. Theatricals were a drug in the market when she arrived. Hundreds of those who draw their subsistence from the Theatre were in a suffering condition. The moment the dancer appeared, the public was roused from its lethargy, and no sooner was life infused into the *heart* of the dramatic system, than the meanest extremeties felt the glow. Thus if she drew from the hoards of the rich, she was the cause of relief to the wants of the poor,—and as some honest people are alarmed lest she should carry off the entire amount of our circulation,—let us ask them—who are the sufferers even if she should leave our shores with $100,000 in her pockets! surely not the poor, for they do not, or should not, contribute any thing to her gains. 'Tis the wealthy then, who enrich this woman. We ask these cavillers whether—if the money were not given to Fanny Elssler—would it be given to the poor! No! it would remain locked up in the coffers of those who now give it, at least, a partial circulation. We would resist 'to the knife' any encroachment, on the rights or interests of the poor—for we are of their number—we are

'Writ with them in sour misfortune's book;

—but we cannot perceive how the most ample support of Theatres, Actors or Actresses can, in any other way than beneficially, affect the interests of any community.

FINIS.

Fanny Elssler in *La Tarentule*.

THEATRE.

The public is respectfully informed that

M'lle Fanny Elssler

Having recovered from the injury received on WEDNESDAY, will appear this Evening in the Ballet of

LA TARENTULE!
AND THE PAS OF
LA CRACOVIENNE!

Last Night but 2 of the Engagement of
MADEMOISELLE

FANNY ELSSLER

Last Night but 2 of the Engagement of

Mons. J. SYLVAIN

Saturday Evening, June 6, 1840

Will be performed, the Farce of

The Dancing Barber !

Narcissus Fitzfrizzle	(a would be gentleman,)	Mr. Chapman
Lord Mincington	(an affected Nobleman)	Richings
Lord Flitterly	(a mysterious Nobleman)	Wheatley
Alfred Fitzfrisick	(an extraordinary Gentleman,)	Nickinson
Mr. Snaply	(an irascible Gentleman,)	Gann
Dunderhead Twaddle	(a pattering Gentleman,)	
Catchem	(a Sheriff's Officer & no Gentleman,)	Milot
Servant		Garland

Gentlemen, Guests, Dancers, &c.

Lady Flitterly	(a fine Lady,)	Mrs. Chippendale
Mrs. Snaply	(a City Lady,)	Miss Cushman
Betty	(a maid of all work,)	Mrs. Pritchard

To which will be added, the Pantomimic Ballet of

LA
TARENTULE.

Luidgi	Mons. Sylvain
Dr. Omeopauco	Mr. Fisher

Notary, Brigands, Peasants, Prisoners, &c.

LAURETTA
M'lle Fanny Elssler

La Signora Clorinda	Miss Bedford
Mathen	Mad. Arraline

Comic Song by Mr. Chapman

After which, MADEMOISELLE

FANNY ELSSLER

Will appear in her celebrated Dance of

LA CRACOVIENNE!

The Evening's Entertainments to conclude with the Farce of

MORE BLUNDERS
THAN ONE!
Or, THE IRISH VALET

Larry O'Hologan		Mr. Shaw
Old Melbourn		Fisher
Young Melbourn		Richings
Trap		Nickinson
Louise		Mrs Chippendale
Susan		Vernon
Letty		Pritchard
Jenny		Miss Turnbull

MONDAY,— MADEMOISELLE

Fanny Elssler's Benefit.

TUESDAY,—

Mr. Hield's Benefit

MADEMOISELLE

FANNY ELSSLER'S

Two last nights of performance will be on
Wednesday and Thursday.

Doors open at 7 o'clock—Performance commences at half-past 7

J. C. House Printer corner of Barclay and Washington sts.

Playbill for the Park Theatre.

Libretto for

LA TARENTULE

A COMIC BALLET IN TWO ACTS.

LA TARENTULE*

This rare libretto was first exhibited at Harvard in The Romantic Ballet exhibition in 1966, under the curatorship of Helen D. Willard. *La Tarentule* was a comic ballet in two acts, with scenario by Scribe, music by Casimir Gide and choreography by Jean Coralli. The première was in Paris on June 24, 1839, starring Fanny Elssler, who also introduced the ballet to London on March 21, 1840.

*Harvard Theatre Collection. Gift of the author.

LA TARENTULE,

A Comic Ballet in Two Acts.

BY

M. CORALLI.

PHILADELPHIA:

Printed at No. 15 Minor Street.

1840.

DRAMATIS PERSONÆ.

————

Luidgi, ...	Mons. SYLVAIN.
Dr. Omeoquaco, ...	Mr. EBERLE.
Lauretta, ...	Mademoiselle FANNY ELSSLER.
Mathea—her Mother, ...	Mrs. ROGERS.
La Signora Clorinde, ...	Mrs. KNEAS.

LA TARENTULE.

ACT I.

THIS Ballet is founded upon the supposed properties of the Tarantula Spider, whose bite is said to throw the patient into a fit of dancing delirium, in which the sufferer expires from exhaustion.

The scene lies in Sicily.

Luidgi, a young peasant, has risen before day-break to serenade his beloved Lauretta; while the merry mandolines are preparing, a band of brigands, forced from their retreat in the mountains, are seen to cross the village, carrying with them their plunder and a lady whom they have, for some time, kept a prisoner. Roused at this sight, the young men run to arms to the lady's rescue.

Lauretta appears, cheerful and happy. Her mother, the rich post-mistress of the village, has told her the

night before that she was to be married the following
day; and the innocent girl entertains no doubt but it
can only be to her beloved Luidgi. Firing is heard at
a distance. The brigands have been defeated, and the
rescued lady shows her gratitude by presents to her
liberator's intended bride. On his refusing any reward
for himself, she informs him that she has power and
influence; and assures him that her protection will never
fail him. She retires under an escort to seek repose in
a neighbouring convent.

A traveller now arrives at the post-house door, a
bombastic individual, the important and wealthy Dr.
Omeoquaco; his presence will soon mar the joy of
Lauretta. Seduced by the charms of the young peasant
girl, the Doctor, whose wife has perished in an encounter with banditti, has offered his riches to Lauretta's mother, and it is for him that the marriage
preparations have been made. On Lauretta's return in
her bridal clothes, the Doctor declares his passion and
intentions, which are disbelieved and laughed at. The

scene, however, assumes a more serious appearance when it is sanctioned by Lauretta's mother; and the unfortunate girl withdraws, protesting that she will never be the wife of any other but Luidgi.

An unexpected occurrence, however, will soon alter her determination. She re-enters, frightened and trembling. Luidgi has been stung by a Tarantula, and she describes his delirium, his frantic dance, and panting agony. No assistance is at hand but that of the Doctor, who, taking advantage of Luidgi's dangerous situation, refuses to exercise his medical skill, unless Lauretta will consent to marry him. The malady is increasing, and if not instantly attended to, Luidgi cannot survive. Lauretta consents, and is led fainting to the altar.

END OF ACT I.

LA TARENTULE.

ACT II.

Lauretta's Chamber.

YIELDING to his entreaties, his attendants have brought Luidgi near to his Lauretta, and, scarcely restored to his senses, her nuptial attire at first flatters his fancy as having been assumed for their own marriage. Lauretta's tears, however, soon reveal the truth, and the painful story is told; a marriage thus obtained by fraud and violence cannot be valid, it shall be annulled. But how can this dissolution be obtained? High protection and powerful influence are necessary; the recollection of the lady's promises occurred to him—she told him that she had power and influence, which would never fail him in case of need. Not a moment is to be lost; the Doctor has already ordered the carriage to take away his newly married wife, and two hours, at the least, are requisite to reach the convent where the lady has retired. Lauretta, nevertheless, restored by hope to her merry temper, promises that for two hours she will retain the Doctor, and Luidgi hastily departs. To obtain the desired delay, the shrewd girl employs every stratagem—now, her friends, by her directions, protract their compliments and the parting glass—now, her toilet for the journey is made unusually long—now she kneels in prayer before the Madonna—then, seemingly frightened by a strange noise, she locks up the Doctor in an inner room; the old man, however, re-enters through the balcony; she is at her wit's end, and not half the time is as yet elapsed, when a ludicrous idea comes to her assistance; she feigns to be stung by the Tarantula, and assumes the depressed countenance, the feverish tremor and frenzy, which she has witnessed in Luidgi's case, and yielding to a fit of frantic dancing, defies the efforts of the Doctor to soothe her supposed madness. Alarmed at this extraordinary effect of the bite, the Doctor calls the company to assist, and Lauretta falls apparently dead from exhaustion. Her mother accuses the Doctor as the cause of her daughter's death; he is on the point of being roughly treated, when Luidgi returns, and, in the lady who accompanies him, the Doctor recognises his wife, whose life has been spared by the brigands. Now, to complete the tortures of the Doctor, Lauretta suddenly recovering, pretends to claim him as her husband. She very soon, however, yields her pretensions, and offers her hand to her dear Luidgi. The Doctor's only alternative is to return to his wife, and the postillion entering the room, reminds him that the carriage has been waiting for two hours.

END OF THE BALLET.

MAD^{LLE} FANNY ELSSLER.

IN

LA TARENTULE

Fanny Elssler in *La Tarentule*.

LA CRACOVIENNE AND LA GITANA,
AS DANCED BY
FANNY ELSSLER.

Fanny Elssler in *La Cracovienne*.

Fanny Elssler in *La Cracovienne*.

Elssler Quadrilles, a romantic montage designed by S.C. Jollie. The center oval shows Fanny Elssler in a Gipsy or Spanish dance, the four corner ovals, starting upper left and reading clockwise, show a Spanish dance, La Cracovienne, La Sylphide and La Gitana.

NO SLUR, ELSE-SLUR;

A Dancing Poem

No Slur, Else-Slur: A Dancing Poem

Verse inspired by Fanny Elssler seldom survived its appearance in newspapers, but this curiously published pamphlet is an exception. This copy has written in pencil, under "By Nobody," the name of James Cook Richmond. He may well have been the author. Mr. Richmond published verse under his own name in 1851, which he had written while in confinement at the McLean Asylum in Somerville, Massachusetts.

NO SLUR,

ELSE-SLUR:

A

DANCING POEM,

OR

SATYR:

BY NOBODY.

[James Cook Richmond]

And Katerfelto, with his hair on end
At his own wonders, wondering for his bread.
TASK.

NEW YORK.
PUBLISHED BY ANY-BODY, SOLD BY EVERY-
BODY, AND FOR SALE ANY WHERE, BUT ES-
PECIALLY IN WALL ST., AND BEFORE
ST. PAUL'S, BROADWAY.
1840.

NO SLUR, ELSE-SLUR.

ARGUMENT.

A Fling at Baltimore—Boston—Philadelphia and New York, touching the Reception —Invocation to two kinds of UNDERSTANDING—Austria—Vienna the happy birth place—Schlegel—Old Proverb—Phrenology and Podology—Cambridge and Transcendentalism—History—Poetry about the Danube—The Muses—Terpsichore and Fanny compared—Fat father, humdrum Yankees—Hard times and hard dollars—Modest difficulties of the description—Praise of the Modesty of American maidens—Young Napoleon—Metternich and his destiny—Arrival—Modest beginning—Innocence dancing—Modesty of the dancing Dervishes—Coney Island—Rejected invitations —The momentous German Serenade—Homily.

SHALL Baltimore the heavenly dancer draw?
Shall biped asses, giving horses law,
Unyoke the chargers from her four-wheeled throne,
Unharness horses' necks to fit their own?
Shall Boston gravity and Boston sins
Melt down before her well-turned, public shins;
Shall great, small, pompous, empty-headed men
Pay scores to see such angels dance, and then
In plausive wonder let the stage disclose
Immortal Fanny running on her toes?
Shall Philadelphia Quakeresses dare
Breathe in the purlieus of the poisoned air?
In this wise drama shall it come to pass
That Fame and Dollars crown the greatest ass?

Must York's sons, matrons, widows, glorious maids
Court, feast, and marry Europe's renegades?
And I not sing? Ye Muses, no! I will
My full brains empty—empty pockets fill.
Does she kick out their cash with pedal *strains?*
I'll win that cash by throwing out my brains.

O UNDERSTANDING! goddess of the crowd!
Thee I invoke by all the plaudits loud
That ever *deafened* ten such graceful toes
As hers, whereon a German dancer goes
Leading wits, fools, and dandies by the nose:*
Thee I invoke; for unto thee belong
The bones, toes, tendons, sinews of my song:
Or else, good sooth, I will (it better were)
Fall down, like other sheep, a worshipper
Of her, chief priestess, of thy *sole-full* shrine
And swear her *understanding* is divine.

FAR as Apollo may excel my songs,
So far the theme excels all mortal tongues.

Lo! all the *mental* powers of *Austria* meet,
And shower perfection on a woman's feet:
O blest Vienna! who has heard before
That thy voluptuous bosom held such store
Of mortal graces? True it is, we knew
Thee unsurpassed in dinners not a few;
(Five times a day Vienna's sons may dine,
Five times a day hot coffee follow wine:)
True that great Schlegel, Criticism's law,
Poured out his life by filling up his maw

---

* Note the climax.

With Austria's sauces and Vienna's wine;
So Schlegel died, where Schlegel meant to dine.

SUCH powers we knew were thine; for long before
Our untaught feet kissed Europe's classic shore,
'Twas sung that Spain *of old*––ye gods! not Spain,
The emblem *was* of Europe's head and brain,
And France the bosom; set that bosom low,
And France, for us, may as the bosom go;
Old Italy, and England *now* her arms,
But thine, blest Austria, were the stomach's charms

ALL this we knew, to Austria honor meet;
But never deemed her *first* upon her *feet*
Till now, when we behold the nineteenth age,
Send such a wonder on the world's wide stage,
That wits and fools and dandies sit entranced
To think how well a pretty woman danced.

O SHADE of Spurzheim! whither flies Phrenology?
Where's now that old new humbug, Magnet-ology?
Where Atheistic Transcendental-ology?
Undone for aye by Viennese Podology!

Our wits, as always, late upon the road,
Catch up what Europe saw long since explode;
If yet you doubt, ask Cambridge, she can tell
How many fragments there from Deutschland fell:
How many notions puzzle *Harvard* men,
That erst in England boggled Carlyle's pen,
And will, we doubt, be mysteries again!
How many wonders mighty Coleridge sung!
He too saw Germany while very young.

My theme demands: in Francis' time at Wien*
A burgher dwelt: such often have I seen
Where glorious Donau† rolls his waters on
Almost like rivers of the setting sun,
Slow winding where the hill of Leopold
Bathes him at sunset in whole floods of gold,
He stays his silver waters calm to see
The far famed home of *modern*‡ minstrelsy,
And bids the boatman from Bavaria's shore
Rest, O blest moment! his forgotten oar,
That midway hangs between the wave and air
Glistening entranced, as if eternal there
Where music fixed it; while the helmsman bends,
And all his spirit to the Syren sends;
And still, as Donau wafts him to his goal,
Gives up to Wien a willing, captive soul,
Nor all her outward glories stoops to see,
Locked up in chains of blissful harmony.

'Twas there, where Prater§ sees the city dame
Walk with her husband—or some other flame,
Was born a child, marked out, by Fate's decree,
More graceful goddess than Terpsichore,
Yea, more, for never have the Muses Nine,
Though Greece and Rome bowed suppliant at their shrine,
Snuffed adoration, Fanny, equal thine.

O Blest fat father! little didst thou know
Thy daughter's feet should bid thy *honor flow*,
Far as a steam-ship in a year can go.

---

* Vienna.　　† Danube.　　‡ The " Poetry of motion."
§ A famous mead near Vienna.

Ye willing nations, come, and bending pay
Such homage to that old man as ye may;
Pay fast, and pay it hard in dollars good,
Which Fanny laughing takes beyond the flood;
O bright Celeste, thy game is understood.

Ye winds propitious fill the *honored* sail!
Let Fanny laugh in Europe at the tale,
And when she sings of fools, the great and good,
" Dear humdrum Yankees there, ayont the flood!"
Be all her songs of praise addressed to thee,
Our city goddess, Gullibility.

LET her not sink with that sweet, well-earned gold,
For which in TIMES SO HARD her dances sold,
By public views which never can be told.
Cannot be *told?* O Jove! I had forgot,
Our gentle damsels go to *see*—what not?
Be not abashed my country-women fair;
The Muse may *glance* at that whereon ye *stare*.
Use you those lovely eyes! use I my pen!
I've *seen* fools dance, nor need to see again.
Once, fool! I thought, thus! thus? you cannot sing;
But lo! small scruples to the winds I fling;
For sure where'er Columbia's sons may roam,
The greatest modesty *is left* at home.
No maidens like America's I see,
Renowned earth-wide for gentle purity,
Which *never* sinks to foolish prudery:
If then our maidens in their daily walk,
Are pure in heart as pure in private talk,
O blame them not for loving well to see
Pure German models of pure modesty;

8

And saw we not a modest painter grieve,
They *paid* not all for Adam and for Eve;
Then surely I am pure who do but twirl
On paper, what they *see*, a dancing girl.

SEE! the Great Western from Bristowa's shore,
Disgorges here what Europe keeps no more:
Pickpockets, murderers, thieves, grace ye my song,
Swindlers, rogues, counterfeiters, fill the throng,
My dancing, *timid* angel, come along;
Fly! Fly! for Frenchmen ask with angry glare,
" Where now is Reichstadt? young Napoleon, where?
" The hope of Europe sunk!"   The Conqueror's son,
By Metternich's Satanic grin undone,
Lies all dishonored, a corrupted corse,
Where erst his father's nod was law perforce!
Such arts of Hell, O Austria, he knows,
Who leads to hell thy princes by the nose,
Until himself straight to the Devil goes.
The time shall come when Metternich must die,
And if he stays from hell, I know not why.

THE ocean crossed, behold, where run the sheep,
To catch of this immortal maid a peep:
And now, how modestly on skilful toes,
She nothing yet but well-turned ancles shows!
Fearful lest Yankees deem her short of clothes.
Cunning, thy name is Fanny! see her then,
By just degrees, the pulse of western men
Feeling with tact, until, in sooth, they find,
Small part of modesty is left behind:
Yet what in secret were a monstrous shame,
When viewed in public plainly asks no blame,

For this good reason: What so many see
Is not the polar star of purity;
But then each damsel taking such small part
How can it harm her tender, youthful heart?
Then Fashion bears them with o'erwhelming tide,
And says, " Dear maids, behold, take Virtue's side.
" See injured Innocence before you dance,"—
Such innocence was far too good for France.

Now, at the threshold, Innocence but half
Displays the glory of a well fed *calf*,
Yet still the dress, by slow degrees, curtail;—
Imagination, come! tell thou the tale.

So have I seen, whilome, in great Stambool,*
Some pious dervish of the Prophet's school
Religious whirl: but in that sacred dance,
The mode displeased me—'twould displease in France:
For while *he* whirled, and dizzy grew *my* head,
Full fifteen minutes—I observed some lead,
Sewed in his fine long robes, did still prevail
To guard his person from the pious gale,
With which so many whirlers there did fill
That ancient dome in Con-stan-ti-no-ple.

The glorious dance is done: now, rest awhile,
Or go with me to Coney's lovely isle,
Let some blest dandy take her forth to ride,
" Dash on, my steeds! lo! Fanny at my side!"

----

* Constantinople.

AGAIN in Broadway! "Will the Fanny come?"
Then ask all Fashion in, rich, new humdru'm,
But ah! for once it proved a greater task
To get them there, than when you gave the masque,
While all New York in February's gale,
Did shivering ask—"Will not their courage fail,
Should death the old man take—or some such ail?"

Now Germany's great sons their homage pay,
And bring such honors as their music may:
Ye butchers, and ye butchers' sons, beware!
Ye blackguards, how with Virtue may ye dare,
Mix up your cruel, blood-stained, gory hands?
With Virtue, such as by yon window stands,
Dancing to Deutschland's serenading bands.

"BUTCHERS and loafers, hear, O hear!"   But no!
"Blackguards"! and "Music."! "Yet no blood must flow
"In vain for me,"! the modern Helen cries:
But all for nought: the brickbats threat the skies
Frequent: and now, midst music's raptured throes,
One gaunt musician misses half his nose,
And oft some eye-bung from the battle goes.
The scattered instruments lie here and there,
But now by Fanny's Innocence we swear,
Such blackguard rowdies did behave unfair;
For Germany's proud thousands would but bring
A serenade to her, whose charms I sing.

MY FATHERLAND! High heaven! O what shall be
In time to come thy doubtful destiny!—
Once there was Hope: long years it was our care
Of this Republic never to despair:

Alas! alas! how shall I, free from blame,
Here drop the song, without one word of shame?
Shame for my country!—shame that she will ape
Each rascal Count who can from France escape:
Shame that my country-women, ever dear,
(When I was far, then to this heart most near;)
So far forget the muddy crimes of France,
As in the mazes of the waltz to dance!
O, if I grieve, 'tis when a lovely maid,
Who should of shadows almost be afraid,
Submits to let some foreign scoundrel whirl
Her maiden figure: O, beware sweet girl!
"The first step costs,"—I tell thee now, beware!
Thy fate hangs here on trifles light as air—
O! didst thou know that atmosphere, like me,
Ball-rooms and theatres should never see
Such heavenly charms, such angel purity!
What! *breathe* the air!—O no! far, ever far,
Be thy pure soul from such unholy war!
Where dandies congregate and scoundrels meet,
Both male and female—never soil thy feet.
For by a soul sincere let me declare,
What holier thoughts may not permit me swear,
I deem thy *feet* dishonored, as they go
Where like a stream our Broadway dandies flow,
A stream impure of "*goats, imperials, curls,*"
And as they go—just heavens! our blooming girls
Seem all unknowing as the million pass,
That near the Astor House they met an ass,
One ass! you cannot walk from twelve to four,
And scape, in Broadway, asses by the *score.*

———

12

My sober song is done—I close the scene;
I've sung, for this time, quite enough, I ween,
Should Fame and Critics disallow my song
The Second Canto will not tarry long.

THE END.

Rare uncataloged American easel print of Fanny Elssler in *La Volière*. George Endicott, 1840.

Fanny Elssler in *The Shadow Dance*, detail from Currier print.

LA DÉESSE,

an Elssler-atic Romance

La Déesse, an Elsler-atic Romance

Fanny Elssler's engagement in New Orleans did not take place until her return from the first winter in Cuba. *The Daily Picayune* reported that New Orleans lived up to its romantic reputation and welcomed Fanny at the St. Charles Theatre in the spring of 1841. J. M. Field, alias "Straws," was the "merry wag" who wrote gossip of the Green Room for the *Picayune*, and was the author of this parody in verse. He wrote skits for the theatre and was, apparently, an actor. On the seventh of April Elssler donated a dance for his Benefit. The *Herald* reviewed Field's "poetic brochure": "Straws is too much straw; but he wants the wheat of the soul—facts, incidents, character, point, wit, scarcasm, and real life. The incidents in Fanny's life, in this country, have been original." Field later tried his hand at a burlesque musical on Fanny Elssler, entitled *Schinder Eller*. It had some success in New Orleans, in spite of the fact that it was written for Elssler's return engagement, which never took place.

LA DÉESSE,

AN

ELSSLER-ATIC ROMANCE.

BY THE

AUTHOR OF "STRAWS."

NEW-YORK:

CARVILL & CO., 108 BROADWAY.

—

1841.

J. VAN NORDEN & Co., Printers,
No. 27 Pine-street.

LA DÉESSE.

Give me a lyre with golden wings,
That with the tone of Eden rings,
That lends the raised spirit wings
To soar among celestial things!
And borne upon its tones away
Enraptured, lost, just as I may;
The angel choirs shall stop and say—
Each chanting Peri, choral Fay—
" Did ever mortal fingers play,
Or soul expand with such a lay!
Stranger! Good day!"

Give me—oh give at any rate
A sheet of *gilt edg'd paper* straight!
Fancy! a little moment wait—
Don't whirl in such a fever'd state,
Thus *pirouetting* in my pate.
One instant!—so—away debate—
The paper!—Now for something great!

La danse ! divine ! ah ! vive la danse—
  Hang it, a thousand thoughts at once
  Are whirling, twirling through my sconce !
One at a time advance ; advance,
Ye witching nothings fresh from France ;
One at a time, from each I'll snatch
Tints that Aurora shall not match ;
Warmth that shall make a tropic bower,
A glorious scene of fruit and flower,
  In ev'ry barren breast around me ;
Words that with poesy's own power
Shall bid the empyrean shower
Down rays of glory by the hour,
  Confound me !

La danse ! No more of music talk,
Through lyrics stray, or epics stalk ;
Painting, deserted be thy walk,
Sculpture, no longer coldly balk
The touch—ye cannot *toe the chalk !*
But thou ! O art with life-blood warm !
Combining each quintescent charm,
Thou breathing marble, bright with all
The tints of pencils magical ;
Whose motion murmurs poetry
In undulating melody ;
Thou spell entrancing, tempting on ;
Thou many muses merged in one ;
Thy reign among us has begun ;
And let the heathen rascal run,
As one too lost to look upon,

Who won't do just as we have done—
Go in for fun!

Within this varied western clime,
Of summer or of winter time,
According as the air is woo'd
In any chosen latitude—
Within this glowing, glorious land!
Where ev'ry thing is great and grand,
Happy, harmonious, and free,
Rejoicing in democracy!
The "States" of course I mean, "the States,"
Sole Eden this side heaven's gates!
Convenient to a certain highland
Call'd "Neversink," and nigh an Island
Not very famous yet in song,
Yet famous too, and known as "Long,"
There spreads a low enchanted bar,
    Where pilgrim eyes delight to look,
There mermaids and a light-house are—
    The "Hook!"

The Hook! the ocean waters bound it,
    And ah! 'tis full of witchery,
Seen from your bark, when coming round it,
    With moonlight on the moved sea.
It shines as every grain of sand
    Were starry atoms sleeping there;
    The light-house, a huge guardian were
Of the enchanted strand!
                    1 *

And fairy sails are skimming by,
   And sometimes music softly floats
Upon the air—for frequently
   They *sing out* from the pilot boats;
And, soften'd by some half a mile,
   " Sam Jones" becomes a pleasing strain ;*
His " solemn oath" begets a smile,
   And ears are lent to list again.
" Sam Jones" the legend to this day
Is chanted upon shore and bay ;
And oh! how sweet the memory
Of boyish days, when carelessly
We stole away from home and rule,
Played " hooky," and deserted school,
To wander, fancy, fetter free,
Among Pomona's treasures, there—
(Heaven, smiling, pass'd the registry—)
To snatch a peach, perhaps a *pair !*
And then, not lonely either, no,
   But with some loved companion ever,
Among the fishing smacks to go
   With bait and hook, a vain endeavour !
List'ning the while to voices, which
   E'er spoil'd, alas, sophisticated,
We thought of quite as sweet a pitch
   As Braham's, he whom hear we late did.

---

   * " It was Sam Jones, the Fisherman,
      Was bound to Sandy Hook ;
      But first, upon an almanac
      A solemn oath he took," &c.   *Old Parody.*

Their strain, the same we mentioned now,
  Speaking of distance-soften'd tones;
He of the " almanac" and " vow,"
  The " Fisherman Sam Jones !"

The Hook ! confound all early lays—
Recalling them, one's fancy strays
Strangely from these less tuneful days.
But, as I've said before, the Hook,
  Upon a lovely night in May,
Reposing, wears its sweetest look
  Beneath the moon's bewitching ray ;
And one who roams upon its sand—
  (I know not if one *does* or not—)
Scanning the lines of sea and land,
Neversink's promontory grand,
  And light-houses, brave beacon spot—
I say, one wandering along
  'Neath such a sky, at such an hour,
The airs of May and ocean's song,
  To lull him with their gentle pow'r ;
'Bove all, if fond of telling stars
  Some hope kept close from mortal ear,
  Or if—a likelier case I fear,
Prone to cigars !
In either case, that lonely one
  Surely feels anything but lonely !
For, poet, he through worlds has run ;
  And if the light-house keeper only,
A thousand thoughts of storm and death
  Contrasting with so mild a time,
Has fill'd his head, spite of his teeth,
  With thoughts of the sublime !

Ah! gaze afar, upon the deep,
   Where sea and sky in silver meet;
A stilly, yet a radiant sleep,
   As of reposing angels sweet!
All, all is one wide flood of light,
Or sea, or air! the baffled sight—
And surely it may be forgiven—
Confounds the brighten'd earth with heaven!

Gaze ye with a bewilder'd eye!
   Seemeth it not a revelation
Of that far, glorious land on high,
   Which saints behold in meditation?
And look! there is a something there—
An object—is't of earth or air!
'Tis shining, but or bird or boat,
Whether designed to fly or float,
Seems just about an equal guess;
Distant, uncertain, bright no less;
And on it comes—what can it be?
   As we have said, the night is calm!
Such airs as live, come fanningly
   From *off* the land, in sighs of balm!
There is a groundswell of the sea,
   Perhaps enough to raise a qualm
Of stomach in some Gothamite,
   For the first time upon the " salt,"
But nought to aid a vessel's flight—
   What can it be?—We are at fault.
A quarter of an hour or so—
   Lord! what have we been dreaming of!

The bright illusion's fled, and lo !
  It is a steamer that doth move,
  Reflecting the fair light above,
    The land unto !

In early times, the fashion 'twas
  When nymphs and goddesses went floating—
(An awkward kind of taste, that's poz,
  But time has much improved their boating,)
The fashion 'twas, in ocean shells,
  And cars of an outlandish make,
To travel o'er the ocean swells,
  Tritons and dolphins in their wake !
A barbarous display in fact,
  Celestial aborigines ;
But modern decencies, exact
  Observance e'en from deities—
No more in " beauty unadorn'd,"
By sea or shore, decorum scorn'd,
They sport devoid of gown or shawl,
A gauze etherial serving all !
They travel with a wardrobe now,
Bandboxes, leather trunks, I vow !
  And mortal-like, content they seem ;—
Abandon'd is the fairy prow
    For steam !
  *   *   *   *   *

There is a crowd upon the deck—
Enthusiasm naught can check—
For *La Déesse !* is *she* not there !
Thrice beautiful in Freedom's air ;

Gazing upon the shining strand
Of that far, long imagin'd land ;
And dreaming of the coming day,
Which shall reveal to her *Broadway*,
Niblo's, the *Park*, and *Battery* !
Painted to her so vividly,
In proper colourings of praise,
Each hour of the last sixteen days !
She stands ! divine one ! Once upon
   A time, when we were young and foolish,
Into a rapture we had run ;
   And now, although our blood is coolish,
We feel its current quickening,
The heart's remains of warmth to bring
   Alike unto our brain and fingers ;
Young love, reviving, shakes his wing,
Just saved from freezing—silly thing,
Dreaming beside an ice-bound spring
      To ever linger.

She stands ! her form, alas, is hid ;
   A crimson mantle, o'er her shoulders,
Approach of night-damp doth forbid ;
   Leaving her face, though, to beholders.
Her face—and, heav'ns ! such a face !
   Description, did it e'er begin with
Features of such a witching grace !
Did Byron, any of his race,
A lovlier dream in any case
   E'er take his *gin* with ?

Her eyes !—but we are bother'd too ;
For whether hazle, black, or blue,
   By moonlight it is hard to tell ;
But whatsoe'er may be their hue,
   Their magic, all can feel too well :
So large, so luminously bright,
Yet with a tender, tranquil light ;
There's pleasure, too, within their gaze,
   For, heavens ! sees she not the golden—
The greatest land in modern days
      By *stars* beholden !

Her nose ! a Grecian, just about
   The thing a nose celestial should be !
And then the lips ! we are in doubt
   If nearer to the mark they could be ;
Not very full, no small confession,
But rounder, lesser for expression
      They would be.
Her mouth ! her teeth ! too wide the first,
   If dazzling pearls were not the second ;
And *they* too many, but who durst,
   Passing such lips, her teeth have reckon'd !
Just such a mouth, as not a soul
Would wish to alter on the whole ;
And whence, a spell beyond control,
      To heaven beckon'd !
Her chin ! ah dimples ! and her neck !—
   But, as we've said, we here must drop it ;
Her mantle throws it's envious check
   Round all the rest, and so we stop it.

But ah! when the returning sun,
Most pleased her form to beam upon,
Shall rise, and all below shall say
That "*La Déesse* is in the bay;"
While GOTHAM shall be emptied half,
Warned of it by the *telegraph;*
Ah! then, among the thousands who
  In extasy shall seek her eyes,
We'll get a good peep at her too—
  Till then, be still'd our rhapsodies.

      *   *   *   *   *

She's come! there's music in the air!
  And fairy voices, whisp'ring, tell
That one as lightsome and as fair,
  Is safely lodged in her hotel!
But ah! if air's delighted race
Said not a word about the place,
  The stranger of an hour would know it;
For ev'ry mortal eye and face
Is lighted with a tell-tale grace,
And tongues, discoursing of the case,
  Lord! how they go it.
She's come! It is not known as yet,
  When, like the blue in April breaking
Through cloud and vapour densely met—
  Or like the morn at sea awaking—
Her radiant presence, bursting o'er
  A scene but lately cold and drear,
Shall chase each cloudy look it wore,
  And get up a small heav'n here!

It is not known, yet in advance,
  Boxes and seats they are demanding;
A day, an hour, and not a chance
  Will be for spots to even stand in!
And Fashion, from her silken couch,
  Where listless she has been reclining,
With Europe's voice of praise to vouch
  The graces now in Gotham shining;
Why Fashion, roused, with eagerness,
Comes from her guarded, far recess,
To lead the crowd—furor—enragement—
And boxes take for the engagement!

A suit of rooms has *La Déesse*,
  Expensive, and of course the choicest;
Embellished with that happiness
  Of taste which round her still rejoicest;
And there, reclining by the hour,
  Which never comes to chase a smile,
The queen of grace, in thronged bow'r,
  Lisps broken English all the while!
But oh! it is not syllables
  Or sentences we care a curse for,
The tone, the music with us dwells,
  And that alone we write our verse for:
'Tis ringing through our bosom's cells,
Like the sweet call of spirit bells!
And then that smile! its winning spells
  We're something worse for.

We have been introduced! Ah me!
  How many for that bliss are dying;

2

Through Gotham, deeply, fervently,
   One warm impassioned wish is sighing ;
In Wall-street groups are gather'd, but
   The talk is not of " stocks," "exchanges,"
Sub-treasurers, or bank doors shut—
   The news more pleasing far, and strange is.
And there is one, behold him ! he
   Of attitude and voice oracular,
One mark'd out for celebrity—
   Who fame acquired with his vernacular !
In childish years, the Ganymede
   Of *Charruaud's* cotillion parties ;
And then the stylish clerk indeed,
   To beat his " Boss" whose chiefest art is :
And next, his own gilt " sign" behold,
" Uncurrent money bought and sold ;"
Versed, on the *town* to make a show,
And *go* ahead as others go :
A speaker at Whig meetings now,
   One of the " Vigilance Committee,"
Bent upon glory any how—
   His name is pasted round the city ;
Or soaring higher at renown,
   With other souls ambition lit ;
Arranging for the gaping town
   A fashionable " Benefit !"
But better, higher, nobler far,
In the bright panoply of war
Behold the hero—born indeed
   Of glory's crowning cup to quaff—
Parading on his foaming steed,
   A Broadway *General* and *staff !*

What more ? Can one thus great, be greater ?
The stock—the " Harlem" speculator !
Successful, famous, followed, trusted,
As suddenly—among the *busted !*

It is a mortifying thing
   This business of *compromising !*
Yet he, the load of suffering
   Bears with a fortitude surprising :
Returned from Europe, just, a trip,
   To aid his grief and health intended ;
In things of taste 'twas his to dip,
   Try pleasure too, he now and then did ;
Had breakfasted with Malibran !
   La Blache, Rubini, Tamburini ;
And, as he hinted, at Milan
   Had taken lessons from Rossini !
At Paris sup'd with *La Déesse,*
And bought a fiddle,—only guess—
   From Paganini !
Behold him ! happy, happy man !
Not envy him, refrain who can ?
Why hath he not this very day
With *La Déesse* driv'n through Broadway !
Is he not privileged to call,
And *doesn't* he *speak French* and all !
A nod from him is fashion, fame,
   A cut from him would be destruction ;
Each creditor would pass his claim
   Paid threefold by an introduction !
The clock has struck, we mean St. Paul's—
And hark ! there goes the City-Hall's ;

'Tis noon, a sunny noon in May,
    The park is cloth'd in early green,
While beauty, floating through Broadway,
    In dyes of ev'ry shade is seen!
Upon the lofty steps, behold,
    Of the " American," or " Astor,"
Groups of the gallant and the bold—
Mustached and strapp'd, of fashion's mould;
    Their glances after beauty cast, or
As often turned themselves to view,
A set of precious beauties too,
    From boot to castor!
The '*Busses* roll by dozens by,
    The cabs, and hacks, half crazy, rattle;
The private carriage solemnly
    Glides on in dignity of cattle;
From Dr. Scudder's opposite,
Six stories high, of marble white,
Fill'd to the roof with wonders quite,
Musicians with their strains invite
The Gothamites of all religions,
Alike to the " *Infernal Regions!*"
And further on, in old " Park row,"
    On " Drury's" step is Simpson standing,
As with Placide he used to do,
E'er " Pompolino" said adieu;
And Peter Ritchings, six feet two
    In stockings standing!
And there is the " Brick Meeting" spire,
Than Peter perhaps something higher,
    But less commanding!

The City-Hall, too, loftily,
Above the trees is soaring ; see!
A glow upon its marble face,
Gives it a sort of modest grace,
As though it blush'd for its inferior
And unillumin'd *brown* posterior !
While Justice, perched high in air,
   And smiling in the pleasant ray,
Seems just as light of conscience there,
   As if it were not " sentence day."

'Tis noon, and ev'ry thing is light
   And life, as we have been describing ;
Each heart is free, and eye is bright,
   For promised bliss all are imbibing !
Behold the crowds, the smiling bands,
   Reading old Drury's " poster " yonder ;
No gazer, sure, but understands
   Their silent rapture, pride and wonder !
" The manager respectfully—"
   Et cetera—the rest we guess.
Three days ! 'tis an eternity ;
How counted will each moment be,
How often breathed in rhapsody
   The name of *La Déesse!*

And now, within her parlour, see—
   We have described it heretofore—
Amid the circle sitteth she,
   Of those permitted to adore :

    2*

And there are beards and whiskers there,
In brave luxuriance of hair;
Mustaches too, and yellow kids,
    And neckcloths of the purest tie;
Coats! but our admiration bids
    Pause, e'er we touch a theme so high!
Collars so delicately small,
    And shoulders padded out so nicely;
Reduced waist, full breast and all,
And skirts of broad and ample fall,
    The thing precisely!
And then such pants! alas, though we
Are singing of divinity,
A deeper inspiration still
Must through our raised fancy thrill,
E'er aught so sacred, so divine,
    So sublimated in the *cut*,
So all transcending, so *dem'd fine*,
    In verse we put!
Mustaches, kids and pants! and there—
    Ah me! yes there are roses too,
Giving their tribute to the air,
    As the cologne they would outdo!
May roses, and sweet violets,
    Devout profusion of *bouquets*;
For ah, what devotee forgets
    To deck the shrine at which he prays.
And thou, renown'd *Grant Thorburn!* thou
Art gathering a fortune now;
"Florist and Seedsman," gentle trade!
Would fortunes thus were only made;

No turmoil, peril, pain, and care,
  Ambition with wild mischief blent ;
And would, for beauty, fortunes were
  Thus only innocently spent!
Music ! yes there is music too—
A soft low voice that ringeth through
The chambers of each bosom there,
And leaves sweet echoes in the air—
A gentle voice, that kindly to
  Some polite question still replying,
Charms with a tone and accent new,
  Language outvieing !

" Mr. Augustus Muffins"—ah !
  Delightful, enter Mr. M.,
The all observed, although his *pa*
  Bak'd " fancy bread" of old—ahem !
But democratic to the last,
Away with pedigree and caste ;
Scorn, as a thing for scorn, we see
Flying the presence of the free.
The elder Muffins !   Who shall dare
Insult the father in the heir !
His " rusk," his " jumbles" famous were ;
  He left an hundred thousand dollars !
Who is there shall contempt declare
  For " krollers !"
Respected Muffins ! faithfully
The city guards thy memory ;
And " fancy bread" hath dignity
  In eyes, perhaps, of all—save one,—
      Thy Son !

" Mr. Sempronius Blather !"—How !
Return'd from Washington ?—Well now !
  A leading man ! a speaker, sir !
  His presence ever makes a stir ;
The " party" couldn't work without him !
  Then he's so boldly honest too,
  Our country the sole aim in view,
'Twould be ridiculous to doubt him.
" Systems are rotten to the core !—
  Corruption !—falsehood !—poisons rank!—
The ship of state, amid the roar
Of tempest, drives on frightful shore ;
Crash ! Freedom, there's but one chance more—
  Secure a plank !
Wreck—ruin—horror—drowning—death—"
  It's plain that Blather is a speaker ;
A man of earnest zeal and—breath,
  Not a mere spouting office-seeker !
He's just return'd from Washington :
  Heav'n bless me ! what's the matter, Blather ?
The ship is sav'd ! the port is won !
  But still you look unthankful, rather ;
Thy eloquence hath sav'd the state,
Thy breath repell'd the storm of fate,
The foremost of the threaten'd crew ;
Is land a more appalling view !
Unprincipled—ungrateful set !
  Once more, wreck, ruin, and disjointment ;
They have refused him—vengeance yet—
  An *unsolicited* appointment.

Another call—and, bless me ! one
Not of the ordinary run ;
A brighter cheek, a sweeter smile,
   A welcome breath'd in softer tone ;
An envious silence, held the while
   By those who wish each glance their own ;
A slight appearance of the sense
   Of pow'r a favour to confer—
Of habitude of deference
   Receiv'd from all, and e'en from HER !
All speak in thrilling whispers to
   That "walk'd over" assemblage, that
A man to whom one can't say "Booh !"
   Puts down his hat.
Who is he ? why he takes her hand !
   Heav'n bless my soul, he even shakes it !
The *usual* shake we understand,
   But this ain't that, and none mistakes it.
And still he holds it—really !—well !—
   While with his left he draws a chair ;
And now, beside her, whispers tell
   Something for which she seems to care
More than the fashionable chat,
So *dem'd* selected, fine, and flat.
Dem it, he isn't handsome ! no,
   And what a *dem'd* cravat and tie !
Not a *demnition* whisker to
   Tickle the dear so *demnibly !*
And then the *dem'dest* coat ! the Lord
   Knows only who his tailor is ;
And *dem'der* trowsers !—curse his phiz,
He's sticking his *dem'd* nose abhor'd

Into her ear again, and half
Inclines the gentle thing to laugh.
Demnition ! cut completely out !
  And some take up their hats to go ;
The rest would follow without doubt,
  But something more they fain would know.
Who *is he ? dem* it, *La Dèesse*
Lacks, can we say it, *politesse ;*
He surely can't a lover be,
Though favour'd thus decidedly,
Yet hath he rous'd a jealousy—
  Such freedoms with a thing divine !
The Lady-killers, plainly see
  That they *can't shine.*
And one by one, and two by two,
They rise, they look, they say adieu ;
Mr. Augustus Muffins, you
Look crusty, but it will not do.
And, Blather, thou, ambition cross'd—
  Neither post-master nor collector—
The smile of beauty, too, engross'd,
  Go hector ;
The anxious time around thee gather,
Cry ruin unto son and father—
        Blather !
And pleased smile, and sparkling glance,
The latest witchery from France ;
And broken English, syllables
  Tack'd sweetly their wrong ends together ;
A faëry grace, such as impels
  A man, somehow, he knows not whither ;

All, all are thine, thou favour'd one,
    And brightly, lightly are they lavished—
Heavens! my pen half mad hath run—
    Ravish'd!
Beauty! when is't most beauteous—eh?
    Some say, when shrinking from the sight
It timidly would fly away,
    Yet by its longings held from flight;
But 'tis not so—it is not so—
    Religion, though none else believes it;
Most beauteous, radiant is its glow,
    When, having bliss to give, it gives it!
And *La Déesse!* She smiles away,
A bliss in ev'ry dimple's play;
And is *he* not transported all—
Turn'd topsy-turvy—held in thrall?
Lord bless me—no! He coolly takes
His hat, and now again he shakes
Her hand, concluding with a squeeze
Should lightning send from heart to knees;
And now a moment's pause, and now,
    Pressing again those fingers taper,
And, with protection in his bow,
    Something he says about his "*paper!*"
An editor! Déesse, divine,
With reason do thy glances shine;
Connected with the daily press!
Smile, smile upon him bright Déesse;
A fitting tribute—and she does—
Her eyes grow brighter as he goes;

They seem to say " you wont refuse me—"
Sweet trust upon her visage glows,
  " He wont *abuse* me !"
    *   *   *   *   *   *

Three hours—it lacks three hours of dark—
  What murmur rises on the air—
The sound of many voices—hark !
  And from the Astor steps, look there !
That crowd investing the old " Park,"
  As if half mad they were !
And Blake has had a busy time,
  The " first tier " gone, the boxes private ;
The " second," " *third*," yet rings the chime
  Most welcome—"places" still they strive at.
And now the rosy day descends—
  The Jersey flats, the bay, and islands
Are bathed in the rich light it lends ;
  Weehawken too, and Brooklyn highlands ;
And, lingering, thy lofty spire
And ball, St. Pauls, are wreathed in fire—
The longing glances of the sun,
That thence, "Old Drury" look upon !
But, *La Déesse*, thy hour is night,
By magic made than day more bright ;
Go, lagging beams, the struggle vain,
Resplendent gas usurps thy reign.

Too eager fool ! we find ourselves
  Scrouged in a corner of the pit ;
While carried out by tens and twelves,
  The fainting fair the boxes quit.

The overture !—oh, agony
  Of pressure and of expectation ;
Hats off—sit down—get up—dear me !
  Toes—elbows—struggle—suffocation ;
The orchestra's invaded, and
  The stage behold them now a cramming :
While, louder than the music band,
  Is heard remonstrance, prayer and d——g !
But what is this which stills the roar,
Which bids the groaning groan no more ;
Which, like an angel's glance below
Into the murky pits of wo,
Bids sound of sin and blasphemy
  Subside into an anxious hope,
That one so rare and heavenly
  Hath come, the fatal gates to ope !
What is it ? La Déesse ! 'tis she !
  As ne'er before, she smileth now,
An angel promise certainly,
  And she hath still'd the row !
An airy, fairy winged thing !
With drapery, untaught to fling
  A veil o'er aught so bright, so fair ;
A film, made of imagining,
  She seems to wear !
As faintly floating round the moon,
By poet seen at starry noon,
A silv'ry mist, a shifting sheen,
Frenzy and love each change between,
      Is seen !
In mazy beauty only clad,
She moves—we're mad !

3

" *Let there be light!*" dear Goddess, we,
It may be thought, go on profanely ;
Yet, full of a divinity,
Why, inspiration speaketh plainly.
And, plainly, e'en as at the word,
Transcending day through chaos shone ;
The pulse of nature sweetly stir'd,
And beauty made each sphere its own :
So, through this dusky, drowsy spot,
Thy advent, ne'er to be forgot,
Was e'en as a divine command,
To stir the lowly, and the grand ;
To light an altar of devotion
In ev'ry breast, or old, or young :
While through the soul these echoes rung,
" Let there be *motion !*"
Motion ! ah, light, and life, and love,
Are lovely, and adorning all ;
But motion, thou art far above
All else which heavenly we call !
Thou'rt even the Almighty breath
Which through the void eternal thrill'd,
When " Light" awaken'd all beneath,
And earth with smiles was fill'd !
Motion !   harmonious, divine—
Déesse ! heed not the smile of pride,
Because this brain is weak of mine—
But, as of old, they deified
Each natural beauty which they felt,
And to its chosen symbol knelt ;
So we, become as pagans too,
Are down upon our knees to you,

As one personifying all
That motion hath of magical !
For now, the spheric harmony
  No longer do we idly dream of;
The heavenly machinery,
  In truth, a part you seem of;
We doubly feel the beauty of
  The countless systems rolling round ;
And, watching yon bright star above,
  Its music we have even found !
The waving flow'r, the bending wood,
  Owning the gentle breezes' sway,
And all that heaven pronounced " good,"
  Hath added charms, since that fair day,
Or rather night, whereon you danced,
And heart, and soul, and sense entranced.

" Hell-Gate !" ye shudder, do ye not—
With trembling hear us name the spot ?
From the bright realm of sylph and fairy,
A cursed change to aught so dreary :
Calm ye—do not alarm yourselves—
Our devils shall be sportive elves:
A fearful place at times, no doubt,
But peaceful now,—the tide is "out."
And moonlight, moonlight—purely down
  An ambient flood all falleth o'er ;
River, or rock, or gray, or brown,
  Or grassy shore.

Tranquillity, the hour is thine;
   There's scarce a ripple, nought around
To break the spell, the " frenzy fine,"
   From " Blackwell's Island" to the " Sound."
No monster steamer rushes through,
   Or "regular," or " opposition ;"
There is a sloop, a schooner too,
But stealthily unto the view,
The nightwind timidly they woo,
     No self volition.
Within the Penitentiary,
In dream, serv'd out their " time," and free ;
Through former haunts the culprits roam,
Unchasten'd by their island home,
   The months of " blasting," and of " digging ;'
Unmindful of what's sure to come
     Of " prigging."
Without, on watchtow'r and on wall,
The sentry's step is heard to fall ;
And now 'tis hush'd, and through the haze
Of pearly light, he bends his gaze
Upon some object floating by—
   Something—that's something like a head—
Or something else—deceived his eye ;
   And hark ! again his tread.
Yonder, on the "Manhattan" side,
Something less doubtful skims the tide :
A barge, pavilion'd, gilded, bright
Within, without, with varied light;
And on it comes with lusty oar,
Illumining the stream and shore ;

While mirth and music in delight,
    Unto the conscious stars are telling,
That there's to be a *fête* to-night,
    Given at the SLIMS' country dwelling !
A *fête champêtre !* all the world,
    The whole world up from town's to be there ;
And some by coaches out are whirl'd,
    And some by boat, there 's one you see there ;
A *fête champêtre*—by the SLIMS !
    The town-talk it has been for days ;
And for a month to come, in hymns
    Of rapture, shall we hear its praise !
Enchantment, on the river's strand,
Welcomes you to a fairy land ;
The grounds, almost a sunny scene ;
    No thought of night or river damps ;
Bowers of beauty—sports between—
In radiance lit, blue, red, and green—
    All Niblo's lamps !
The magic land Aladin found,
As we remember, under ground—
    The gem-fruits on the golden trees
Less gloriously gleam'd around
        Than these !
And that fair mansion ; Mr. Slims
    Had put it up in " '36 :"
A man superior to the whims
    Of fashion and its costly tricks ;
But, having ridden on the flood
To fortune, why, as others should,

3 *

As we ourselves would—if we could,
He built at "Hell-Gate," not of wood,
    But bricks.
"Stucco'd," its colums since have shone
Loftily in the eastern sun ;
Model, the famous Parthenon,
    Minerva's seat, and—Mr. Slims' !
Of all the *temples* round, not one
    But it bedims !

The guests, the happy guests are come ;
    All the " F. F.'s " have been invited ;
(Not understood, perhaps, by some ?
    " First families " ye dull, benighted.)
Five hundred invitations, and
    Oh happiness ! oh, triumph rare !
SHE ! La Déesse—enraptured band—
    Consents to be among them there !
Hearts beat as though they were afar
    Unto a brighter orb translated ;
Star treading, gazing on the *star*,
    Their brains are lost, intoxicated ;
While all the ladies, compliment
    Poetically paid to *her ;*
En costume—upon pleasing bent,
    The *Déesse* petticoat prefer !
The " Déesse sandal" " Déesse hose"—
    The " Déesse garter"—" bracelet"—" zone"—
Sweet hope, by painting like the rose,
    To make its perfume too their own.

J. Courtnaye Snevles ! the *pavé*
    For years he hath adorned well ;
Of thy " five shilling side," Broadway,
    Each flag-stone can his footsteps tell.
J. Courtnaye—the initial J.
    Standeth for John, and some might sign
Plain John C. Snevles, not so he ;
J. Courtnaye—makes a dashing line,
    While John sounds rather snobbishly ;
Besides the flow'rs of poetry
    Hath it not his been to entwine—
    Within the Mirror's self to shine
        D—d fine ?
" Lines by J. Courtnaye Snevles," yes !
Touching, oh, plaintive M., no less
        Than thine !

J. Courtnaye Snevles ! fashion and
    The muse, behold, combined in him
With person, six feet does he stand—
    The *statuesque* of breast and limb !
And rich, and courted—all has he ;
    E'en beauty, formed to wooing wait,
A pleader has been known to be,
    While his is still the " single state."
J. Courtnaye, though, thy time is come !
    The lion in the toils, at length,
Contemplates placidly his doom,
    Nor seeks to use his strength.
Déesse, it is to thee he bows,
For thee the airs receive his vows ;

He saw thee, and his captive heart
Bade freedom, with a smile, depart.
His was the first bright wreath that fell
   To crown thee on that fateful night,
When first 'twas ours to view—to tell
   Of thee, the graceful and the light!
His, also, was the diamond hid
   In roses, with his card attached,
Which on the next occasion did
   Salute thee brightly, thou unmatched!
And his, too, were the verses, writ
   On paper sweetly scented, tinted;
Which told in music he was *smit*,
   And at his soul's deep wishes hinted!
His, lastly, is the gilded barge,
   Twelve oared, and canopied in state,
Which touches now the shining marge,
   Bearing thee, Déesse, to the *fête!*
God bless thee, little archer boy!
   Wounded or healed, bliss or pain;
Willing to crown, or to destroy,
   We reverence thy reign!
Who fears thee? not the sorest heart
That rankling, bears within, thy dart;
The weeping eye, the throbbing breast,
The hopes thou, smiling, witherest;
The innocence, the ebbing life,
   The last, fond, still deluded sigh;
To thee, forgot the wrong, the strife,
   Clings trustingly!

How the happy moments fly,
Each one more deliciously ;
How the many-colour'd light
In gay devices greets the sight ;
How the flatterers are inspiring,
How the flatter'd are admiring ;
How they dream that they no less
Are worship'd than thyself, Déesse !
How the fountains are a-flowing,
How the barges are a-rowing,
How the waiters are a-glowing,
How the ices are a-going,
And hark ! there are the cocks a-crowing !

J. Courtnaye, hanging on thine arm,
Ev'ry sense to warm, to charm,
Is that divine one, La Déesse !
And thou art envied, thou may'st guess.

Ever bland, her smiles now blander,
Sweetly with him does she wander ;
Farther, farther yet away
From the festive scene they stray ;
Far from lamp or watching eye,
Save the heavenly ones on high ;
Far from mirth or music's sound,
The conscious trees alone around ;
From rivals far, and rivalry,
J. Courtnaye—thou art on thy knee !

"I love thee, lovely—loveliest—
    I own six houses in Broadway!
A fire—a flame is in my breast—
    I am distracted—rich I say!
Six houses!—Eighty thousand I've
    Got of my own—this throbbing heart—
It's true that *Pa* is yet alive,
    When gone I get the larger part!
Two hundred thousand—all on thee
    I'll settle—love distinction levels;
Distraction—thou divine one, be—
    Rapture!   Mrs. J. Courtnaye Snevles!"

Hail mystery! we love thee well,
Thy presence hath a nameless spell;
Unseeing, thrice sought is the show,
Unshowing, wild the wish to know.
J. Courtnaye, what hath come of thee?
Echo says "what?" mysteriously.
But from the Mirror of last week—
    And every week it brighter shines—
Conveying what we would not speak,
    We copy these mysterious lines:

THE BLASTED ONE!

By J. Courtnaye Snevles, Esq.

I.

Ashes art thou my blighted brain,
　And burnt my blasted brow!
A thought of fire through ev'ry vein
　Like blazes scorches now!
A riven wreck, upon the plain,
　A ruin standest thou!

II.

They say that beauty is a mask,
　That woman's words are wiles;
That any man should rather bask
　In sulphur than her smiles,
And that the love he'd better ask
　Of scaled crocodiles!

III.

Too true! howl on the desert wind,
　Flare fearfully the flash;
Oblivion's gulf, I rush to find—
　Dare fate pronounce me rash;
Tis here—one spring—Death, thou art kind,
　Here goes at once—*slap dash!*

And hours and days are gliding on,
And thou, Dèesse, bewitching one,
In admiration's ardent blaze,
Unscorched, art passing hours and days.
It is not that thou can'st not love,
   But where is that refined earth,
Celestial sympathy to move,
   And love call into birth!
And days and hours are fleeting, and
   The moon is in its *gibbous* state,
And does not rise, you understand,
      Till late.
'Tis up, long after midnight, just,
   That is, if the " Hall" clock is right—
And it we're bound of course to trust—
   Three hours beyond the noon of night.
Dian, on roof, and spire, and dome,
Smiles sweetly from her azure home;
Her glorious domain above,
   Where, mistress of the starry train,
Amid her court of light and love,
   She rises, smiles, and sets again!
Yon vast hotel—throughout the pile,
   Halls, galleries, and countless rooms;
One does not mark a taper's smile,
   A window where a wick consumes,
And some uncounted hundred souls—
   Infant to aged, black and white;
Thy sway, oh mystic sleep, controls
      Quite.

Love, fame, and wealth, revenge perhaps,
(For, ah, there are such savage chaps ;)
In varied shape invade their rests ;
  Soothing or vexing—mystic dream,
  Of Heav'n or hell 'tis thine to seem,
  As brains with calm or care may teem,
    Or food digests !
One chamber—from on high, a ray
Delighted thitherward to stray,
And kissing all in silv'ry play,
  Peeps gaily through the open shutter ;
Illumes a couch whereon there lies
A form for moonbeams made, not eyes ;
Whose charms, but sylphs in rhapsodies
  Alone might utter !
A form—enough, a gentle form,
All nicely covered up, and warm,
Particularly so, as snug
As ever bug within a rug ;
It being not too hot nor cold,
  Nor sultry airs, nor chilly creeping ;
But " temperate," none need be told
  A night for sleeping.
And sleep she does—she smileth now,
  As if a seraph harp she heard !
And now a sigh—oh ! ask ye how
  The leaves in Paradise are stir'd ?
I'd say, the holy bowers of bliss,
When echoing an angel's kiss—
  For that they kiss we have inferr'd—
Are moved by sounds e'en such as this
  Upon my word !

4

She dreams, she smiles, she sighs, but what
   It's all about, we're left to guess;
Of one beloved—or may be not—
   Certain it is not of distress.
And now, upon her gentle side,
   She, restless, turns—disturbs the cover;
Which never in its whitest pride,
   A whiter neck has covered over!
She sighs! and hark! responsive to
   That faintly fleeting melody;
A strain of music echos through
   The chamber, sweetly, joyously!
She wakes,—she hears,—she lifts her head—
   She listens with a pleased surprise;
Is dream, or magic round her spread?
     She rubs her eyes!
Louder it rings—she *is* awake—
It must be so, and "no mistake;"
And now she turns the cover down,
   And out a rosy ankle slips;
And loose and lovely—do not frown—
   Across the floor she trips.
She's seated at the window, and
   She peeps through the half open "blind;"
And now, a strain, full, gushing, grand,
   Mounts on the morning wind!
Lord bless my soul! a serenade!
A genial tribute, gently paid;
But hark! what sudden sounds are these?
   The strain is broken off!—
Or "wind," or "string," their harmonies

Are hushed, the sweet " flute passages,"
  Or trombone's cough !—
And there are fifty instruments,
  And music desks, all ranged and lighted ;
A gather'd crowd—and what prevents—
  What hath affrighted ?
Discord !   dark " wizard of the glen,"
  Thou of the " magic scarf," accursed,
Thy foulest caves, the souls of men,
  Thou'rt come to do thy worst !
Enough to urge thy fiercest ire,
That SHE is here, and men admire.
" Down with the fiddlers"—"Douce the glims"—
  " Smash—smash the fiddles," is the cry ;
And sweet Déesse, thy peerless limbs
  'Scape not indignity :
" Hurrah for heels"—and " go it legs"—
Thus venom spits its poison'd dregs ;
" Break up the benches"—" burn the books"—
  And " brass-blower"—and " catgut scraper ;"
" D——d squally " the whole matter looks—
  " Douced" ev'ry taper !

And thou, J. Courtnaye Snevles, thou
Art there, spectator of the row.
What ! art thou not the champion knight ?
Defend'st thou not sweet beauty's right ?
With soul of fire, and arm of might,
Mak'st thou not one amid the fight ?
Alas, that we should say it, see !
With folded arms, all gloomily,

With pleased vengeance in his smile,
   Remorse chok'd in his puff'd cigar ;
And glancing at yon " blind," the while,
   He views the savage war.

But, gallant Muffins ! 'tis not thine
   To idly stand, or e'en *back out ;*
" Vive la Déesse !"—" live the divine"—
   In French and English hear him shout !
And, valiantly, with hooked cane,
   His instrument he seeks to guard ;
A "grand piano"—borrow'd—vain—
   The hate of hosts he cannot ward.
'Tis one of " Chickering's," and on
   Two wheel-barrows, together lash'd,
'Twas brought to lend its sweetest tone—
     It's smash'd !
   "Bass," "double bass," and "first," and "second ;"
" Horn," " hautboy," " flute," and " clarionet ;"
" Drum," " trumpet," all, surprised, beset,
   Bruised, broken by a foe unreckon'd ;
They flutter, falter—gods ! they fly—
Shouts the triumphant enemy :
   The " watch," *in time to be too late,*
   Pause at the cry—they hesitate—
And peeping the Park railings through,
And seeing the defeated crew,
As careful watchmen ever do,
   They leave 'em to their fate.

" Down with the dandies"—cheer and cheer,
  " Uptown," triumphant, fills Broadway ;
Down Barclay-street, in route and fear,
  Apollo rushes, all dismay !
Hold !—There is aid, ye flying ones !
  What music, valour could not do ;
La danse ! to conquer Discord's sons,
  Has been reserved for you !
Why pause the victors ?—why is hushed
  The shout of rage, the cry of fear ?
The madness to and fro that rushed—
  What hath transfixed it here ?
Yon window—open thrown the " blind,"
What lovely vision floats behind—
The moon-beams on their radiant track,
With added brightness, throwing back !
'Tis she ! and smiling, smiling still !
  And raised aloft her snowy arms ;
A hush of rapture—a deep thrill
  Subdues the wild alarms !
Hark ! a familiar, charming sound—
A deeper stillness falls around—
" *Crack !*" has an ear permitted been
  To hear, and ever to forget—
An Andalusian dream within—
  Thy spell, sweet castanet ?
From katydid, or cricket's throat,
Ne'er came a more peculiar note
      We'll bet !
She waves her arms, and gracefully
Her head, her neck in harmony ;

Her bosom, also, she is bending—
" *Crack !*" Hail *Cachucha*—maids of Spain !
Motion !—thee we pronounce again,
   All else transcending !

J. Courtnaye Snevles ! after all,
No triumph thine, to ease thy gall ;
Discord ! defeated, homeward crawl ;
   And see the spirit whom you hate,
By beauty, and by grace alone
Supported, on her rosy throne
   Reign, lovely and elate !

Déesse, say, do you take the papers—
   Or English do you read at all ?
Heed ye the editorial capers
   Which your delightful capers call ?
Or, pocketing your "thousand" nightly—
   Laden with roses and applause—
Say, sit ye down to supper lightly,
   Your bosom ringing with hurrahs ?
We don't know what you think of it,
   But oft we've thought they serve you sadly,
As far from reason, ev'ry bit,
   As they who rave about you madly.
You're a delightful creature, Fan !
   With pearly teeth, and raven curls,
   And stag-like bounds, and fairy twirls ;
   And fooling with such kind of girls
      Upsets a man !

But, setting foolery aside,
   Fair one ! how look you upon life—
Its flattery, abuse and pride ;
   Its brief repose, its lengthen'd strife ?
No woman ever more than thee,
From sweetly down to bitterly,
(We think,) hath tasted of its stream,
'Mid shadow, well as sunny beam ;
Never unto a woman's lips
Hath offer'd been, more frequent sips
   Of that sweet mixture, admiration—
With slander's bowl, whence poison drips,
      Mingling damnation !

Déesse ! you must have soul and heart ;
   They speak in your unmatched grace :
E'en if in eyes where heav'n hath part,
   E'en if in your repose of face
We saw not a full share of either,
   We'd see it there—a certain case—
Nor questioned neither.
You've sensibility ; and say—
   Is it offensive most, or funny,
The fulsome jingle of the day ?
   Or doth the jingle of the money,
Incessant as it is around thee,
With its too potent spell confound thee ?

We don't believe it !—coming are
   The hours when roses wan and wasted
Shall mock, however placed by care,
   The empty cup, too fondly tasted !

We don't believe but there are springs
  Within thee swelling, freely, purely,
And that affection's angel wings,
Checking the flight of darker things,
    Protect thee surely!

We don't believe a single word
  Which robs thee of a charm—believing,
And seldom, seldom have we err'd,
  Howe'er they talk about deceiving—
We don't believe but future hours
Will bear thee brighter, sweeter flowers;
Will bring thee still a golden store,
And of a purer, richer ore—
The treasure of a mind at rest!
  Our pray'rs are brief, as you may guess,
But brief and earnest, are the best;
And if such ones are ever blest,
    You're "all right," sweet Déesse!

ELSSLER QUADRILLES.

Elssler Quadrilles, a romantic montage by Ch. Zeuner. The roles portrayed are, reading from the top and left to right, a Zapateado, La Gitana, a Spanish dance, La Tarentule, La Cracovienne, La Sylphide.

THE
LIFE
OF THE
BEAUTIFUL AND ACCOMPLISHED
DANSEUSE,
MADEMOISELLE FANNY ELSSLER,
OF
VIENNA.

⚬⚬⚬

THE EARLIER PART OF HER LIFE COMPILED FROM
"BELL'S LIFE IN LONDON,"
AND REPLETE WITH ANECDOTES RELATED BY AN
ENGLISH GENTLEMAN,
LATELY FROM LONDON; AND ALSO FROM A NUMBER OF THE
AMERICAN PAPERS.

SELECTED AND COMPILED
BY
A LADY OF THIS CITY.

Printed for the Purchaser, and for Sale, wholesale and retail, at No. 65 Walnut
street, Philadelphia; No. 141 Fulton street, and retail at the Big Tree,
Wall street, near the Custom House, New York.

Title page of *The Life of the Beautiful and Accomplished Danseuse, Mademoiselle Fanny Elssler of Vienna.* The Library of Congress.

La Cachucha.

Fanny Elssler and Mons. Sylvain in the *Pas Styrien*.

A Short and correct sketch
of the Life of Mad'lle.

FANNY
ELSSLER

A SHORT AND CORRECT SKETCH OF THE LIFE OF MAD'LLE FANNY ELSSLER*

This "short and correct sketch" of the life of Fanny Elssler by Peter Pindar is a boiled down version, often word for word, of the earlier, spurious life of Fanny by "A Lady of This City," here identified as "A Lady in New York." Its inclusion in this collection of souvenirs is sufficient to illustrate the penny-terrible fiction and the pious humbug published during the anti-Elssler campaign.

*Boston Public Library

A

Short and correct sketch of the

LIFE OF

MAD'LLE. FANNY ELSSLER.

(THE CELEBRATED DANSEUSE.)

Containing:

A condensed history of her birth—her career as a danseuse—her illicit intercourse with the young
Count Reichstadt, and other Noblemen, up to the present day.

BY P. P.

....

PHILADELPHIA—For sale at No. 11½ North Sixth Street, (up stairs,)
and in NEW YORK at the well-known stand in Wall Street.

PRICE SIX CENTS.

TO THE PUBLIC.

The subject of this little memoir is the celebrated *danseuse* Mad'lle. FANNY ELSSLER. Much has been written and said in relation to the *divine* Fanny—some have attempted to laud her to the skies, and o hers to excite public indignation against her—neither one nor the other of these, however, is the object of the Author of this little sketch, and he has gone to considerable trouble to procure the *facts* upon which this narration is founded, and which are principally from European *Court Journal's* and *Bell's Life in London*, and a work published by a 'Lady in New York;' all of which can be relied on as truth. Hoping that it may find the approbation of a kind and generous public, I subscribe myself the public's

Humble Servant,

Philadelphia, July, 1841.   PETER PINDAR.

Mad'lle. FANNY ELSSLER is the daughter of a highly respectable Merchant, of the Imperial city of Vienna, where she was born sometime in the year 1816; she received a good education as her family was wealthy, as well as respectable. As dancing is her forte, and her parents having judgment sufficient to discern and cultivate her youthful talent, as they were conscious it was in that *only* she would acquire peculiar excellence, placed her at an early age under the best master Vienna produced, from whose unremitting attention and instruction, she derived such rapid improvement, that at five years of age, she excited the admiration of every one that had seen her, and she v as pronounced the most graceful figure that had ever been exhibited in the science of dancing. This improvement in her favorite art, so gratified her affectionate parents, that no expense was spared to render her a proficient in the cultivation of the graces, and their expenditures was amply repaid, at the early age I have mentioned, when they seen her move like a butterfly, over the floor of a brilliantly lighted Ball room, the fairy "Queen of Night;'—while love for the beautiful child, and admiration of her extraordinary proficiency in the elegant art, to which she was so devoutly devoted,

> While wonder filled the mind,
> To see a baby thus inclined.

How much greater was their exultation on arriving at a proper age, to know her move the most admired *belle* in the "corps of Terpsichore," on the Vienna Opera House boards, she being then both a beautiful, well formed, elegant, brilliant girl. Having been compelled to appear before the public to remunerate her father for her education, he having been unfortunate in his business, or the lovely Fanny had not been a *danseuse*. That, maugre the deficiencies of liberality in the fancy Fanatics, that Supreme Being, who decides over the fate of dancers, as well as those pious persons, extended his divine mercy to Fanny, and rendered her the admiration of Europe, as before she had attained an age to seek the patronage of a generous public, she was compelled to accept the terms offered her by the Manager of the Vienna Opera House, to pay the debt of gratitude due to her parents, for their extraordinary expense in her education; thus her brilliant talent as a danseuse, enabled them to support their usual genteel establishment, as her annual income from the Opera House was liberal, and the public justly generous, from a consciousness that a sense of paternal duty had brought her before them, therefore her *benefit* was always an overflow, or, as an English writer should say, a *"bumper."* Thus she continued to improve both her fortune and her fame, enjoying the approbation of her own head and heart, in thus cheering the declining age of her parents, by her dutiful conduct, and acquiring by practice the perfection in her profession, which is so peculiarly her own. Years rolled on; Fanny became a blooming beautiful woman, if possible more elegantly brilliant than in her early days of childhood, when she had only held out the promise of that excellence, to which she has now so happily arrived. These halcyon days passed gaily over; life to her was the brightness of a summer's day, for she lived only,

> To rise with the lark,
> Who soars on fancy's wing;
> Or the fairy group,
> Who gaily dance and sing,

Beloved by her fond parents, admired by the proud nobility of Vienna, what had Fanny to wish for; nothing but love—and to that she ever turned a cold and soul thrilling heart. Fame she had gained, and fortune she was acquiring by the proceeds of her profession, and then she had not another wish ungratified. This ambition was fully satisfied; nightly was her services required, and she was the chief magnet of attraction to the house, to all ranks of people of Vienna,

> Who feed her thirst for fame,
> And gained her an immortal name;
> Her compeers wondered as they gazed,
> At the sparkling brilliance of the stage.

Thus joyously, happily, and respected, passed the first years of pretty Fanny's entering in her teens; beloved by many, old, middleaged, and young; the ancient and middle-aged for her virtues and dutiful submission to her parents; and by the young, for her beauty, talents, accomplishments, good humor, and generosity. Thus honorably and delightfully till the age of sixteen, when the means of exerting her generosity on an extensive scale, towards any age, sex, or country, was immaterial to Fanny; all alike, past the days of Fanny; she had her bounty; this generous system of benevolence, so extensive, endeared her to the citizens of Vienna, generally and the Nobility, nay, even to Royalty itself, that she was looked up to with both respect, admiration, and wonder, all ranks strove to emulate each other in rendering her benefit a source of monument to all parties, as the knowledge which they all possess, that a lovely girl, scarcely past the days of childhood, not only supporting her parrents in ease, comfort, and elegance,

> Yet chering the hearts
> Of many a child of want.

This bore her fame to the most remote corners of Europe.

> The poor look up to her,
> And call her blessed.

Such numerous virtues and talents, combining in a young and beautiful girl, dependant on the public for her support, attracting the attention of many a hoary, though rich *libertine,*

> Who strove by every art to win
> This blooming beauty into sin;
> But all in vain, for their shame,
> Bright Fanny kept pure, her virtue

4

She took their presents, read their letters, laughed at, then destroyed them, and rejected their offers with silent contempt. Fanny continued on thd highest pinnacle of fame, of virtue, beauty and philanthrophy till she attaine- her sixteenth year. Dancers in all countries, and in all ages, from the dance ing girls in Asia, to the most celebrated *danseuse* in Italy, Spain, France, Germany, England and America, are by the seducers in all ages in these countries considered as public property; therefore are they admired, fol- lowed, flattered and caressed till they fall; and how terrible is their deviation from virtue, not only to themselves, but their parents also! Their honest lovers, if they have any, and their public fame, are all sacrificed to the vile betrayers. Fanny could have married an honorable and worthy man, had not temptation assailed her, in the person of the young Count Reichstadt.

Who has not heard or read of the great Napoleon Bounaparte, the Con- queror of Italy, and a large part of Europe, and Emperor of the French, or of his *ill* assorted marriage with Maria Louisa, daughter of the Emperor of Austria; and in the son of this man the beautiful Fanny Elssler met her seducer, in a youth of scarcely of mature age; this, and her extreme youth is the only extenuation of the art with which she eluded the vigilence of her ever watchfull father. Fanny had from her entrance into public life been accustomed to see the youthful Count Reichstadt, occupying his august mothers box in the Opera House, and receiving from his eyes that approba- tion of her performance etiquette forbid his yielding in the usual manner to her grace, elegance and surpassing beauty, their eyes had met in the moments of delight and exchange; glances each felt, but neither understood.

The Count's looks of love, were, by the proud Nobility of Vienna, impu- ted to approbation of her unrivalled tatents, ease, elegance, and grace; thus each soft smile towards him spoke volumes to his heart, while the multitude that surrounded them fancied it was humble gratitude for his condescension, in bestowing on her a look of approbation, was honoring by his presence her performance; but as none understood those glances of love, sacred only to lover's eyes, a heart on which they doted in their closets — nor would any of the proud nobility have credited, had they been so informed, that the love they coveted for their daughters, sisters, nieces, or grand daughters, should be the property of a public dancer, the child of a merchant, what, though he had been once afflued, he was at present poor, and dependant on that duti- ful daughter, who was herself obligated to the public for their patronage; such a suggestion was deemed prepostorous, and none could have ever convinced the exclusives of the fact. To the *elite* it was an embryo which time only would bring to life; but what can escape the eyes of the politician —nothing—and the cunning politician who detected their love in its early stages, fed the foolish passion, as it was generally supposed, but to allure the count to destruction.

Prince Metternich watched the progress of the fire, which was secretly consuming the hearts of the two youthful lovers, and privately fed their folly by imperceptible steps to the precipice of ruin, from whence he hurried them down the gulf of shame, from thence he could hurl them at pleasure into the abyss of misery and death. He was at last too fatally succesfull When the prince first intimated his discovery to the Count Reichstadt, his blushes and evasive answers confirmed suspicion and he secretly resolved to the ruin of both these interesting young persons, the Count, and pretty Fanny, and succeeded, but too fatally, in maturing the secret folly, he had detected in the Opera House, when blooming, in all the bewitching charms of sweet sixteen, artless, innocent, and admired, her beauty embellished, by the elegant costume so becoming her countenance, beaming with love and pleasure, that she appeared to the young Count's fancy as one of the favorite Goddesses, or a wandering Sylph, who had descended from the airy abode of the regions of light, to charm his every sense, rather than a dancing girl, who was exerting all her talents in the graceful art, to delight and amuse him; while she, impelled by the passion that glowed in her breast, excelled even herself, on that fatal night, when her charming smile, on quitting the stage, gave the Count hopes of success, disclosed, their mutual passion to the profound politician, well knowing that they were then at the most critical point of all periods in the life of both sexes, yet maugre feeling, honor, pride, and self-respect, without pity, or even sympathy, with a fond and doting widowed mother. and conscious of the pangs he must create for the good old Emperor, who adored his only amiable grandson, basely to initiate himself into the Count's confidence, and extracted imperceptibly the dearest, as the young man fancied the best concealed secret of his heart, for which he repaid him by indulging his *amour impropre*, with the graceful *danseuse*, and condescended to act as pander to the youthful pair, at whose secret meetings he connived, till her ruin was accomplished, and the Count secured; whether he secured the secret apartments in which they met, was not known, but at the Count's request, a house was purchased for his beloved Fanny, or rather, a *villa*, where he could pass a few delightful hours, or even days with her, and she reside, free from the prying eyes of Nobility, and the authority of her parents, whose distress and grief, at her fall wrung their hearts with grief, and anguish, to whom she transmitted money to support them in their elegant establishment, which they uniformly, and resolutely refused choosing to submit to every deprivation, rather than live in elegance, on the wages of their daughter's shame. Fanny thus placed in a charming villa, a short distance from the busy haunts of men, I might add the impertinent curiosity of women, enjoying for a time the most perfect happiness, loving and beloved, her hours passed in raptures, when visited by the Count, and during his residence with her, all was sunshine; but this was for a brief season;

> Too soon did death assert his sway,
> And call her heart's first love away.

Thus, bereaved of her idol, totally without the Christian's hope of meeting in a better world, poor Fanny was, for a time, almost a maniac; it was then the tender parent, forgot the errors of their suffering child, pressed her with fondness, forgiveness and commisseration, conducted the suffering victim of political intrigue to their humble home, where the mourner was for a time concealed from every pursuit of her enemies.

The next account I read of her, she was at Paris, pale, spiritless and dejected, she looked no more like the blooming Fanny Elssler, that had delighted many of the French nobility in their visits to Vienna, in her bright days of youth and innocence, and though the expression of her countenance was sad, there was a pleasing sweetness in its pensive cast, that in a measure atoned for the loss of her brilliant bloom. The French generally seem to possess a greater charm for banishing sorrow and care from the bosom of affection, than any other nation. This power was, I understand, successfully exerted in Fanny's favor by all ranks and degrees, and in short her former beauty, cheerfulness and health returned. This improvement in her circumstances contributed, in no slight degree to render her an object of attraction to the young dissipated noblesse of France, who sought her society, with all the assiduity that passion and galantry could practice; again was Fanny assailed with letters, offers of settlements, the richest diamonds of Golconda, with every temptation that could be invented, to entice her again into the paths of destruction. But in vain did her Father watch; her Mother pray. In vain did Fanny, as heretofore, return their letters, and reject their offers. In vain did she assure those insidious young men, who, by bribery and stratagem, obtained access to her presence,

That her her heart was cold to love, as Alpine snow,
Or ice that on the Andes grow.

The next *successful* assailant Fanny had was the Duke of Orleans, who called personally at the residence of Madame Elssler. He humbly asked permission to see her daughter in *private*; but this her mother promptly refused, and the Duke left the house disappointed and dejected. Where there is will there is always a way, says an old proverb; and his grace of Orleans soon found the way, through power of gold to obtain an interview with Fanny. For a while her heart was cold to his love, and averse to his proposals; but who can resist royalty, beauty, elegance and love, when combined in the person of a noble, fascinating young man,

Whose eye allures, and whose tongue persuades.

Fanny could not, Thus tempted again she fell; Fanny had been raised in a city, habituated from infancy to all the luxuries and elegance that a profitable and extensive business can produce and at a more advanced age she had been placed before the public in a conspicuous situation; being flattered by the patronage and plaudits of the crowned heads of Europe. She had been the chosen object of an ardent enthusiastic young mans love; and had not his rank prevented it, an honorable and legal attachment, this passion would have made her his wife; it had not passed lightly from her bosom; these circumstances, combining with her dread of solitude, where she was conscious she would only weep over the fallacious hopes, and death's cold joys, till madness might ensue; for Fanny loved not solitude; as to her,

Green fields and shady groves, with bubbling springs,
Larks, woods, and nightingales are odious things;

she fancied there would be more happiness with a charming Duke for a companion, an elegant villa for her residence, within a short drive of Paris, and a retinue of servants for her attendants; so thought, and so acted Fanny; for on her father's return to Paris, he found her mother weeping at her daughter's secondary dereliction from virtue; and Fanny established in an elegant Villa, such as her fancy had portrayed, whither he followed her; but prayers and tears were all in vain, she persevered in her constancy; by this time, Love, the sly urchin and master of arts, had sent a dart at fair Fanny, and her liason with the Duke which had been formed by circumstan stances, became a passion, and she loved the Duke with a feeling if not as tender, ardent and durable, as had been her attachment to the Count, still it was warm enough to satisfy the Duke, and for a time they basked in loves sunny bowers, surrounded with elegance, the idol of a fond Nobleman, who lavished thousands on her; she was now patronizing, when before she was patronized, giving to the poor with a liberal hand. Fanny was happy for months, and her present amour, like all other ILLICIT engagements, was, for a while, so immured from society, and engrossed by the company of her dear Duke, who seemed to live but for her, that she was entirely lost to the world; but this happiness was not to last. The liason between the Duke and Fanny was abruptly dissolved by the then convulsed state of Europe, and the marriage of Leopald, King of Netherlands with the Princess of France.

In the next place, 1833, I find her engaged at the Opera House, London, her : Fanny might again have gained confidence, for the nobility of England will tolerate and pardon genial errors, when not practiced under their inspection ; but I am sorry to say that the favorite forgot honour, prudence and delicacy—for according to the work, from whence I derive my information, I find her dancing to attract the attention of an elderly gentleman of high rank, and vast fortune, with whom she afterwards formed a liason, although he was a married man, and old enough to be her Father. What her inducements were to place herself under such protection, no one could imagine ; her salary was liberal, her patronage was extensive, and of the first order in the kindom; therefore it must have been her mercenary motives alone, which influenced her to form this connection ; if so, her views were fully realized, as her establishment was elegant, her jewels splendid, and her dresses the richest that Paris could furnish : this engagement lasted till decency required him to attend his lady to the German Spa, for the recovery of her health.

And in his absence, Fanny coquetted with any young nobleman who chanced to make overtures to her; and they were numerous that sought her society, no doubt on account of her amorous qualities, and which she now used to every advantage. Fanny's beauty had created her many enemies among the subordinates of the Opera House, and her frailty gradually reached the Dukes ears, and the liason was terminated shortly after his lady's death: and for a time *the* Elssler was the most fashionable *belle* of the season. *Lover* succeeded lover, in her favor—and being totally void of art, or not caring to conceal these flirtations, which were marked by her enemies, and reported accordingly, by this folly she lost the favor of the court.— Hereafter her illicit liasons in England were numerous, and she would on the discovery *faux pas*; or even flirtation of hers, withdraw from the English stage till such were partly forgotten, and she was again recalled. On such occasions she generally made an excursion to Paris first, the scene of her second error, where she was ever received with the most unbounded applause by the nobility of all ranks, and citizens of every class and situation; her liason with his grace, the Duke of Orleans, had not depreciated her in the estimatiod of the liberal-minded Parisians ; and her return was always hailed as a jubilee, by the patrons of the Opera House. Her residences in

8

that city, was therefore, even to her, a source of pleasure with profit, and it was with regret she quitted Paris, to fulfil other engagements, which she had made previous to her leaving England, with the various cities of Europe.

Madlle. Elssler was a dancer, young, beautiful, with a heart formed for love alone; she was, therefore, by the young nobility of Europe, marked as a proper object for dishonorable pursuit, and as such was she sought for, by dissolute libertines of those cities, where her profession called her; for alas! she had 'no brother in a sister's quarrel bold." Her father, when she formed the liason with the duke of Orleans, consigned her to her fate, and cursed and renounced her as a stigma to his name—and Fanny continued travelling from one city to another, whither her profession called her, as though she preferred that wandering life to seek for a permanent home, and for nearly five years she had no other accommodation than the Inn's in which she stopped in her several journeys, and the Hotels which accommodated her, when stationary during the period of her performance. At length however, she resolved again to visit Vienna, the place of her birth and her first deviation from the path of virtue, she being at the time without either engagement or liason, After remaining in the city privately and secluded for some weeks, she at length met her mother and sister, and a reconciliation between them took place shortly after. Here Fanny again engaged in a liason with a young and handsome Nobleman, which was continued during her stay in Vienna. Both Fanny and Therese made an engagement at the Opera House in London shortly after, which was completed with success, honor, pecuniary advantages and the highest *eclat* possible. After this Fanny made the engagement with the late Stephen Price, then one of the managers of the Park Theatre, New York, which brought her to America.—

Fanny was received with great *eclat* in this country, and success has attended her in every city which she has visited, and will continue so during her stay with us. Report says that she has since her sojourn among us, been under the protection of Mr. W. of this city, but whether this is the case I am not able to say. She has, I understand, made an engagement with the managers of the Chesnut Street Theatre, which she will fulfil sometime in August next, when all those who have not yet seen her, will have an opportunity to behold the greatest *danseuse* of the age !

Fanny Elssler in *El Sapateo de Cadiz.*

Fanny Elssler in *La Sylphide*.

The Letters and Journal of

FANNY

ELSSLER

The Letters and Journal of Fanny Elssler

Henry Wikoff wrote the *Letters and Journal*. This is not publicity: here is no barker. It is the kind of good reporting in letters which the roving diplomat Wikoff wrote all his life in articles to the press. Three installments were first published in *Fraser's Magazine*, London, in December 1843 and January and February 1844. The editor, in a preface to the first installment, made it clear that the work was not from the pen of Fanny Elssler, but it did contain her impressions of the many charming and interesting incidents during her travels.

On February 15, 1844, Fanny Elssler wrote the *London Times* from Milan, publicly disclaiming all connection with these articles, as she felt that they were published with the intention of making her appear ridiculous. The editor of *Fraser's* answered Fanny's letter the next day in the *Times*: "Previous to the publication of the first paper I received a letter from Mr. Henry Wikoff (who is now on his passage to New York), in which he wrote 'Mademoiselle Fanny Elssler gave me, a year since, a full and unqualified assent to publish her travels, and she has never withdrawn that assent.' "

The *Herald* in New York presently copied the articles from *Fraser's*. James Gordon Bennett reported that the dancer had repudiated writing the articles and added: "It does not much matter, since they are interesting, that the articles have been written by Fanny's *chef de cuisine*, Henry Wikoff."

Fanny Elssler's travels were of sufficient interest to be published anonymously as a pamphlet.

THE

LETTERS AND JOURNAL

OF

FANNY ELLSLER,

WRITTEN BEFORE AND AFTER HER

OPERATIC CAMPAIGN IN THE UNITED STATES.

INCLUDING HER

LETTERS

FROM

NEW YORK, LONDON, PARIS, HAVANA, &c. &c.

NEW-YORK:

PUBLISHED BY H. G. DAGGERS,

No. 30 ANN-STREET.

1845.

FANNY ELLSLER

AT

PARIS, LONDON, NEW YORK, AND HAVANA.

LETTER I.

RESOLVES TO VISIT AMERICA—PROFESSIONAL CAREER—PRIVATE LIFE—THE MEN OF THE PRESS—JULES JANIN, THE AUTOCRAT OF CRITICS.

PARIS, November, 1839.

MY DEAR MINA : A good while has elapsed since last I wrote to you ; it is not to be wondered at, for you know the busy life I lead. What with theatrical duties and private engagements I have scarcely an hour to give to more congenial tasks—to writing, for instance to you, my dear Mina : but I shall make up past neglect by sending you such "news" to-day as will indeed rouse you, and scare away for months to come that ugly little imp of *Ennui* which sits brooding over your monotonous life in quiet, placid, stagnant Berlin. Your active mind and ardent feelings want something fully to occupy them ; and that you cannot find in the tranquil employments of a purely domestic career. Yet how often I long to change lots with you ; for there is in me a deep-settled relish for the calm routine of an in-door life, utterly at variance with the feverish excitement of Parisian society. It shines brightly enough to one's admiring friends ; but, ah ! it consumes while it glitters. Would that I could arrest but for a moment the rapid, noisy torrent that hurries me on, if only to speculate *where* it will leave me ! But a truce to reflections, let me come to the "news" at once. Well, Mina, I am about to cross the Atlantic and proceed to America ! I dare say you have heard of some such place, but, like myself, have a very indistinct notion of its whereabouts. Now recover your breath, that wonder has, doubtless, quite taken away, and I will do my best to explain this wild whim ; for, in truth, I cannot look upon this strange intention as other than a mad freak that has seized my fancy in a thoughtless moment, and has daily grown into shape, owing to the doubts and opposition made on every side against it. My sober judgment could never have brought me to such a resolution. I appreciate fully all the advantages and enjoyments of my position; it would be exacting and ungrateful not to be contented. Have I not all that any reasonable woman, if there is such a being to be found, could desire? My professional career has reached its zenith; here I am, sitting securely on an operatic throne, that has dazzled my eye and fired my ambition, since my girlhood. *Le grand monarque* never swayed more completely over the wills of his admiring subjects than I do over the rapt fancies of my enthusiastic admirers at the Opera. Never was *artiste* more completely seated in public sympathy, undisturbed by rivalry, unassailed by critics, and popular even with that formidable foe, the *claque*. The curtain is drawn, and I appear, to be welcomed with smiles that make the theatre glow "'neath their sunny warmth;" I dance, and rapturous applause cheers me to loftiest efforts; I curtsey, and flowers and garlands cover me. And then the delights, more intoxicating still, of the *entre-acte*. I quit the scene for my *boudoir*, whose silken splendor owes all its elegance to the taste and liberality of my kind *directeur*. What do you see, Mina, in its sparkling mirrors? What a gay, gallant, and graceful throng encircle me, occupying every chair, besieging every sofa! And have I not reason to be proud of homage from such a *levée*, representing the rank, the wit, the elegance, of this brilliant capital — the white-gloved denizens of the *avant-scènes*, whose "bravo" is the fiat of our scenic fate?

More potent and majestic ones than these I pass respectfully by; and of the rest, every one worthy of the privilege, I will single out for your admiring attention some of those "dreadful few" who seem proudly conscious of their importance, and of our trembling accountability—the critics of the press. Amid flatteries, compliments, and adulation, one grows giddy with the strong incense, and fancies one's mastery complete over the spell-bound crowds within and without. One forgets places and things, and revels in the luxury of undisputed despotism. Am I not downright mad, you ask, to trifle with and to contemn such enjoyments, as these? I have nothing to wish for, you say—nothing to disturb my illusions. Gently, dear sister, you forget the "tribe" I was just writing of. I do taste of sours as well as of sweets, for these messieurs of the press often write rudely, in order to dispel one's fanciful dreams, and so melt all down to the chilling reality of a helpless subjection to their invincible domination. Ah, these men of the press! the terror of their craft; doubtless they are meant to secure some good end, else why do they live and prosper? The enlightened friends of art, and foes to all oppressive authority, I hear them styled, when I have sometimes murmured at their usurpation; but how impossible it is to hold power without abusing it, and how cruelly do these enemies of absolute control tyrannise over us poor *artistes!* A thoughtless word, an absent look, an idle jest, may seal our luckless doom. Should their high displeasure be incurred, what would be left us but the loss of position and bright renown—all we have and all we hope for—and thus are we bowed down in abject submission! But whence, then, arises this reluctant allegiance to this feared and relentless power? Will no one ever come to redeem us? Will no modern Joan d'Arc raise her banner of revolt, and head an Amazonian band to exterminate them? But I must be prudent, for I have never rebelled against the supremacy of the critics without soon after having good cause to rue it. I do not wish to live a victim, nor die a martyr; and, to be serious, then, there are those among them whose graceful pens would extort one's admiration, even in a malicious assault upon one's last new *pirouette*. Come back again, then, to my dressing-room, for you have much to divert you there. Join in the racy chat, contribute to the smart fire, so well sustained, of *bon mot* and sharp-set *raillerie*.

Your eye is resting (I thought it would) on that droll-looking person, lolling at his ease in yon *fauteuil*, disordered in dress, careless in manner, and yet imposing, spite the tangled locks that fall in sad confusion over his ample forehead; that is the Coryphæus of *feuilletonistes*, the very Jupiter of the tribe. His thunder-bolts fall among us at times with killing effect, but he can also give life to an *artiste*, and make it priceless; that is "J. J." of the *Journal des Debats :* I wonder at my temerity in approaching so calmly his formidable initials, so often signed to the epitaphs recorded on our artistic tombs; but his indulgence to myself emboldens my familiarity. He is chiefly known to the public for hebdomadal contributions to the famous *Debats*, wherein he empties his effervescing cauldron of critical remark, all steaming, hot, and spicy. He makes the tour of all the novelties the week brings forth, and then on Monday morning disburdens his memory and his conscience. Like the immortal hero of *l'Elisir d'Amore*, he dispenses his doses with prodigal hand—a bolus here and an elixir there; administering to wounds of his own making the soothing ointment of his praise, and in very wantonness scratching others half healed up. But rail, rant, and roar at him as we may, who can shut their eyes to the brilliant, sparkling, seductive light of his genius, winning while it repels, delighting even when it chides, intoxicating when it extols? Yes, Janin, I believe an *artiste* never fell beneath thy rod who did not kiss it while it smote; for it lashes so beautifully. This singular person is the theme of constant remark; his eccentricities (for it seems genius must have them,) his peculiarities, and *penchants*, furnish endless gossip to the "Foyer."

His last new predilection now sets all tongues a-wagging; and who, or rather what, do you dream is the tender object of his love? He has taken to a pet; and what, of all the things of air, earth, and sea, do you imagine has won him? Oh! name it not in Berlin—"a little pig!" with doubtful claims to whiteness. Byron had his bear; Goëthe his monkey; and Janin fondles a pig! What is the attraction of this new caprice; what the sympathy between "J. J." and his darling, who can tell? The topic is prolific in *bon mots*, to those who dare make merry at his expense. "Yes," exclaimed the lively Comte de ——, the last opera night, "there must be mutual feeling from similarity of pursuit; the pig scours the street of its offal, and Janin ranges from one end of the Boulevards to the other for his theatrical garbage." Wo to the bold jester if this comes to Janin's indignant ear; he will avenge promptly the outraged dignity of his *petit cochon*. All societies are open to Janin. the court invites him; his numberless friends prey on him; the dinner languishes, the soirée is dull, the representation is flat, when Janin is not there. Hunt Europe through, and you will not find another man more courted; and the same journey over again would not discover you an equally successful competitor. The *coveted* of *artistes*, the *dreaded* of dramatists, and the most gifted of critics, how shall I support the loss of thy vivacious effusions—the delicate embroideries of thy style? Pirouetting will lose its charm when "J. J." is not there to criticise. Bless me, dear Mina, how tiresome you must think me in prating so long of a good-for-nothing critic you care little for! In talking of Janin, I have allowed all my company to steal out of my *loge* without a parting smile. Well, fancy the curtain's up again, and the music waiting, the director impatient, and Katty scolding. Write me soon. Adieu!

LETTER II.

Paris, December, 1839.

Dear Mina—I cannot help smiling when I think of the undisguised astonishment you so honestly express; but you have given me an unexpected token of your disinterested devotedness to my interests, by the impartial comments you make in reference to my "foreign project." But you can hardly believe me in earnest, and want naturally enough to know what has already taken place—some particulars, details, proofs, that the "*pays sauvage*" I talk of visiting is not some new "*mise en scène*" in a forthcoming ballet of the Grand Opera; in short, you want to see the wheels of the new theatrical car building for me, to, to be sure it can move. *Dieu* grant I may not be upset in it! When the proposition was first made to me, I really cannot tell. A year ago, I know, propositions were suggested to me in London by Mr. Seguin, the clever theatrical agent of Regent street, whose dexterous manœuvring with us operatic dynasties makes me regard him as the Talleyrand of his art. His experienced eye saw in the measure many advantages. I was incredulous and indifferent, and so the matter dropped. But, in August last, I was surprised by the visit of no other than the lessee himself of the Park Theatre, New York—an oldish person, stout, and cross-looking, stiff in movement, slow of speech, with a very sharp eye. I was not, you may imagine, conciliated by his appearance, though gentlemanly; but his offers were business like and ample. Still nothing was decided on, and he left Paris, requesting a friend to urge the negotiation. The matter went on till it took the formal shape of a written agreement, which, one day, I was asked to sign. I began to tremble, and I shrank from the consequences; but I had given the interview almost for this purpose, and courtesy forbade me to trifle with the patience of others. So I took the offered pen, and wrote my name. I shall long remember the confused emotions which seized me when I did so. I felt as if I had pronounced my own exile from a land I love, and a public who lavish every kindness upon me; but it was too late, and I am condemned to expiate my rashness in what manner soever Fate ordains. I must not forget to tell you a droll incident connected with this contract. It was made in accordance with European usage in the main stipulations; but I learned, from the honorable explanations of the opposite party, that I had forfeited some most desirable advantages; in fine, that I was at the mercy of the foreign lessee, when I ought to have reserved the most complete freedom.

Here was a discovery! imagine my agitation! Bad enough it was to encounter the chances of the enterprise, but to begin by heavy sacrifices! What was to be done? My friends assembled in council; every effort was made to alter the agreement. I besought it almost with tears in my eyes; but entreaties were vain. "It could not be done," Mr. —— said, "without the consent of Mr. Price, then at New-York; he should be written to straightway." This is a bad eginning. Is it ominous? Do encourage me, Mina, for every one assails me here. I should make exception, however, in favor of two remarkable persons I have had the singular good fortune to meet—Mr. and Mrs. G——, of London, of high position, great fortune, and a circle of friends embracing all the celebrities of their wonderful metropolis. I am amazed at the deep and earnest interest they take in me, and I acknowledge with delight, that, in this late difficult business, their counsel has much aided me. Their kind interference greatly benefitted me ; we have become quite intimate ; and I never felt more solicitous to retain the friendship of any one I have ever met than I do that of the G——'s. Mr. G—— is a very *distingué* person, but somewhat reserved, as Englishmen of that class usually are ; given to Latin, Greek, and literary occupations ; is writing a great book about I don't know what ; and leaves his wonderful wife to occupy herself about me. Truly, of all the women I have ever met she interests me most—I might say of all persons ; for men, *you* know, divert me but little. They are a vile set altogether—coarse (but don't tell 'em I say so,) selfish and unbelieving. How little do they understand me ! What a relief, then, to encounter such a woman as Mrs. G——! so full of true sympathy, elevated feeling, and kindheartedness. Of her mind, I will not aspire to speak ; it is very far above me ; but when I see her holding lofty discourse with men profound in thought, and great in reputation, with statesmen, authors, scholars, I feel timid in approaching her. But with me she is as playful, simple, and unsophisticated, as a child. She is older than I am, and taller, with an intelligent blue eye, of a soft expression, a little stiff in manner, perhaps, at first, but singularly decided. She never crosses the room without her mind being made up to do it. She's a striking mixture of the two sexes. With a heart truly feminine, she unites the

mind of a man of genius ; and this latter gives her a boldness of thought and expression which quite startle her hearer. But the most captivating point in her character is her truly catholic spirit, looking tolerantly on the world, and perceiving good in everything. She soars above vulgar prejudice, and, in her benevolent flights of feeling, hesitates not to light on spots from which more timid birds would fly, and to fold her protecting wings over objects often worthy her fostering care. She is also most marvellously accomplished, has studied music as a science, draws admirably, paints charmingly, and drives four-in-hand. Let me see, what is there she does not do ? To know such a person, whom I have rather caricatured than portrayed, is in itself a privilege ; but to be loved and cherished by her, is a boon of inestimable value. I have tried to make you comprehend my English friend, and you will often hear of her from me.

I dare say, with your usual activity in such matters, you have been buying a map with America drawn on it, and its rivers, and mountains, and towns ; for I suppose it has got its share of those necessities that most countries stand in need of. Do tell me something about it. I don't believe my stupid old schoolmaster ever heard of it, for he never told me any thing of it that I recollect. I know a great deal more of the moon ; at least I have seen *that*. When shall I behold this unknown part of our planet ? I ought to be ashamed of my ignorance, no doubt, but I see wiser people about me who never wish to know of any place out of Paris—the world's epitome. There are some complacent Parisians who doubt the existence of Germany at all, or, at the most, admit there *may be* such *barbarians*. Every day I hear some acquaintance ask of America, " Qu' est que c'est que cela ?" Then how should a poor dancer, whose travels have been chiefly confined to the Opera-house, who has crossed rivers with the aid of a mechanist, and scaled mountains by running up some hidden stairs, be expected to know anything of a half-savage land, thousands of miles away? I have no time to investigate it now, for my school-days are over, indeed, before they ought to have begun. My day-life now is but a rehearsal of what I must play at night; and therefore, dear Mina, I count upon you to enlighten me upon this dark subject, and to tell me where I am going.

Since I wrote you last, I have had a new sensation, and I must try to make you share it with me. I have seen an American! of whose authenticity I can hardly doubt. Some of that name have been pointed out to me before, but I have always taken them for Englishmen; and they are wonderfully alike—talk the same language, dress similarly, and doubtless eat and drink after a similar fashion. This person, Mr. C——, is a soft-mannered man, of most winning demeanor, and well-bred in every word and look. If he is not a too fair specimen of Americanism, I shall have nothing to fear for my throat or my pocket; though I have been assured I may count on the one being cut, and the other picked. Mr. C—— tells me the news of my intention has reached America, and has made quit a stir there; that the people are talking of it, and the papers writing of it. Oh! dear, I had fondly hoped there were no such things there. I wonder how they treat us dancing things. *Nous verrons!* I was assured I shall meet with a hearty welcome and with great success. How strange this sounds! Were I to get a message (I speak it not profanely,) from the other world, that preparations were making to receive me there, I should hardly feel more puzzled.

My final representations here are announced at the Opera, and I feel flattered to see the public crowding up to look their last upon me, not for ever, I trust: Heaven forbid! One may well be pleased who feels she exercises *some* influence here in this charming Paris, amid the endless and seductive variety of amusements with which it abounds. I feel, with reason, gratified, if not vain, of my influence over the lively throng that ebbs and flows, in such heavy tides, through the great doors of the Opera-house. You ask me how I can summon up courage to leave a sphere that you are pleased to say, I " brighten with my presence —when the gayety of ballet will be eclipsed by my departure?" Thank you for your sugared remonstrances, my dear Mina; but, though I feel my star in the ascendant now, I know well the fate of " stars " once gone out, people soon learn to see by other lights, and then all those here, and elsewhere, will twinkle brightly enough for my now devoted public.

As to my delightful contempararies and coadjutors, I believe their tears will dry rapidly. I will confess, too, that I have certain misgivings that I shall be supplanted. The public may take offence at my apparent ingratitude in quitting them " *pour les sauvages d'Amérique,*" as they style the unknown people I purpose visiting, and they may satify their tastes with some newer object. " *Qui quitte sa place la perde,*" is an old proverb that keeps dancing in my eyes till I grow impatient. Some of my *adorateurs* assure me daily, that they will bespeak their tomb-stones if I insist upon going, and that the *loge infernale* will be hung in crape. Irreverent jesters! they would be the first to forget me, and the last to welcome me back again. Yet I ought to be grateful to this formidable band, this " Conseil de l'Opéra," since they have uniformly issued their solemn and scented decrees in my favor, though I do not like their intrigues and arbitrary interference. Yet their tyranny is a well-bred one, and their fashionable sway may control coarser influences running in a rapid undercurrent in the troubled waters that us operatic naïads sport in. Yes, all this I risk, all this I shall miss, but how much more there is beyond the confines of the Académie Royale that I shall think of with deepest longings. Oh! dear, delightful Paris, how shall I bear thy loss! thy memory will haunt me ever, and, go where I will, thy image will lie hidden in my heart. I never yet have analysed the secret, but magic charm, that makes Paris the most attractive city of the world. Be their prejudices what they may, come but once within reach of her Circean spells, and an endless captivity follows. Why is this? What part of us does it so *enslave*, that the philosopher or the voluptuary bow alike to its domination? Is it the mind, the heart, or the *stomach*, which are enslaved by Parisian influence? Is it her science, her charities, or her *cuisine*, that wins and subdues all, of every creed, cast, and clime? I have seen enough of other capitals to know the superlative merits of Paris. Her amusements, how infinite and varied! her *artistes*, what talents, and what excess of them!

Opera, tragedy, comedy, farce—in what equal perfection do they exist! A Grisi transports, a Persiani subdues, a Rachel inflames, and a Mars soothes, while a Levassor and an Odry convulse you with merriment. These sources of pleasure are palpable as they are irresistible; but there is something beyond this. What is the mysterious oil that gives such exquisite smoothness to this social machine structure? I believe it consists chiefly in the perennial gayety, the mercurial lightness, the buoyant good-humor of the French character, as developed in the metropolis, for I find the French, out of Paris, quite another people.

I suppose, my dear Mina, you will scarcely recognize in these criticisms the style and manner of your own Fanny. Be it so. At least these are my thoughts and impressions, and it matters but little to thoughts the language in which they are clothed. Adieu.

LETTER III.

COSTUMES—FRENCH MANTUA-MAKERS—THE DIRECTOR OF THE OPERA—VISIT FROM ANOTHER AMERICAN—PROFESSOR VESTRIS—MADEMOISELLE MARS—ENGLISH FRIENDS—THE ADVOCATE LEDRU.

PARIS, January, 1840.

THANKS, Anna, dear, for your prompt replies; and so, giving me full credit for the honesty of my intentions, you doubt my going after all. I have already found that I shall pay dearly for the joke if I do not. I have been laying in such a wardrobe of delicious costumes; upon my word, I have spent a third of my time lately in dressing and undressing. I have appeared, certainly to the satisfaction of Cousin K——, in all the robes of my *repertoire*—*she* declares they are perfect. And in a woman's love of novelty I have been spending such sums, that if America don't help me to pay I shall have to dance at the Prison Ste. Pelagie for the especial delight of the false economists who are there expiating the folly of similar extravagance.

But what a luxury is spending money in Paris! this paradise of women, whose brightest spirits are its dressmakers. What taste, science, and imagination, they throw into the lovely creations of their dexterous hands. Taking this art as a type of civilization—and why not? how immeasurably does its perfection here throw all other places into the shade. My own pleasant friends of the press may say what they please of their influence on the times, but that of a French mantua-maker outruns theirs illimitably. All Europe is tributary to their control, and their dicta can be neither disputed nor denied.

My personal expenditure lately has induced me to reflect (which I do sometimes,) on the enormous expenditure of the opera administration in the one item of wardrobe. Are you aware that they furnish the *artistes* with every article of dress, from a hair-pin to a shoe-string, with every intervening *mystery* of the female toilet from powder to paint? You emerge from your carriage at the stage-door of the opera, in a sombre *robe-de-chambre*, to be converted, by a touch of the wardrobe keeper, into a sylphide or gipsy, wings and tamborine included, at the whole and sole expense of the direction. They do you up in the most complete and radiant manner, as bright as the reddest rouge and the whitest muslin can make you, and all you are required to find are your own smiles and *entrechats*.

When you take into consideration the six or eight first dancers, the dozen or so of coryphées, and the capering legion that constitute the *corps de ballet*, you may then infer the outlay necessary in tricots and petticoats. Then think of the consumption in satin shoes; I seldom use less than three pairs every night, and the slightest soil condemns them, and that upon the dirtiest stage in the world, purposely kept so to avoid slipping. These opera-shoes are of such peculiar make, uniting a certain stiffness with the most perfect *pliancy*, that only one man in Europe has been found with genius adequate to the work—Jansin de Paris.

No wonder poor M. Duponchell,

my amiable director, looks grave and reflective at times. I feel a kind of remorse at the expense I have been to him. How could I have insisted on the additional 20,000 francs in my last contract just renewed? I feel so penitential that I could dance a week for his benefit. What a horrid situation is his! Besides his expenses and anxieties, what endless torment we inflict on him! He is, of course, our high *court* of appeal; and never-ending difficulties and squabbles grow out of the rivalries, and jealousies, and intrigues, that abound in this fairy region of malicious nymphs, and backbiting sylphs, whose wings fail to raise them above this terrestrial propensity, and which give our good-natured director occupation enough to try his gallantry. I dare say he prays that in the next world he may never see a woman, be she angel or otherwise.

M. D. opposes my going, and is disposed to buy in my *conge*, which he has the right to do; but he does not believe, I am sure, that I will *go*, so he will not risk his money. I do earnestly hope my departure will be no loss to him. He has ever been kind and indulgent to me. His humanity struck me a few nights back. In the ballet of the *Gipsy*, I was obliged to put on the Cracovienne costume in three minutes, and return to the stage and begin. A moment's delay would have thrown the orchestra into confusion—it was so arranged, and I was obliged to do it; but the effort was so great that I fainted afterward, on one or two occasions; when he promptly commanded this *rapid* change of costume should cease; and altering a ballet is much more difficult than walking on your head, for right or left you touch the part of some indignant coryphée, who stands or dances upon her rights, and Monsieur le Directeur is forced into all the wiles of ingenious diplomacy.

I have had the pleasure of meeting another American to-day, of high standing, Mr. T——, and was most favorably impressed. I know you think me a very fastidious observer of men, but at least you will admit me to be an impartial one. I have had opportunities enough to arrive at some knowledge of the tribe ; and if, of the number who have flitted by me, you knew the very few that have not provoked indifference, or excited feelings not more flattering, you would very likely be astonished. The American I just alluded to is rather cold in manner, slightly tinctured with haughtiness, but is a high-toned man. All he said had great weight with me, and he guaranteed me, also, a kind reception in America. There is one peculiarity I perceive already in the few Americans I have met. They seem to entertain, and certainly manifest, a deference for our sex, that must be founded on a higher appreciation of women as such, and a more genuine respect for their feelings and characters, than one is usually accustomed to meet with.

Busy as my life has hitherto been, I never went through such a round of occupations as circumstances now entail upon me. What with dancing, and rehearsing, dining out, entertaining at home, sitting for painters, and trying on for dress-makers, writing, studying English, and getting ready to go, you may suppose I am well occupied. *I* never worked harder than I have done this winter, and that chiefly to soothe the keen anxiety of my dear old Professor Vestris. You have heard me seldom speak of this interesting person, whose professional reputation formerly filled Europe—the once brilliant *dieu de la danse* has dwindled, as we all must, into wrinkled and decrepid age ; and his only delight now, he declares, is to play the fiddle as I practice daily before him. This is his only occupation, and he declares he lives his past life over again in me. I confess, with gratitude, my indebtedness to his genius, taste, and vigilant attention.

When I came to Paris, I thought I had reached the topmost round of my art. I had exhausted already every

known difficulty and invented new, but I saw Taglioni and grew alarmed. I felt the ordeal through which I had to pass would be final and might be fatal, for the standard of *la danse* I found so much higher in France.

Fortunately for me, Signor Vestris became interested in me, and endeavoured to raise me up to his own lofty ideas of the art. For three months I toiled as a galley slave before I would *consent* to appear. The very expectation that prevailed frightened me to greater efforts, and the enormous strides I made in advance taught me, that in the dance, at least, one's education is never finished. It was not so much in elementary studies that I gained from Vestris, but rather in style and tone. He sought to give me grace and expression ; in short, *his* finish to my poses and carriage—and the triumphant success of my *début*, he said, repaid him a thousand times. I shall never forget his despair when, after my sad illness of 1836, he found I had certainly *lost my art*. You recollect my prostration was so complete that I had to be taught to walk again ; but when I essayed to dance I found to my horror, that I was utterly incapable of executing the commonest feats of the *foyer*. With desperation in every limb, I sought, day after day, to recover my lost facility. Vestris soothed me and encouraged me by turns, till he groaned and wept over the dreadful apprehension that all was lost. This went on for weeks, when one memorable day I felt a sudden and magical return of my force, and with *a cry* of delight I bounded into the air and danced till I fell breathless on the floor.

Vestris's joy exceeded even mine ; the old man recovered a pupil, and I was restored to the dearest passion of my heart, *la danse*. For its own sake I have pursued it ; the hardest toil has been sweetest recreation, and when I have sunk from excess of practice, I recovered only to begin again. Vestris cannot comprehend in the least why I leave the Grand Opera, the very summit, in his eyes, of all earth-ly glory. He regards England as semi-barbarous, America he does *not* recognize at all ; but when he thinks that what he has condescended to praise is to be given to " savages and negroes," for he believes, with a great many else, that America has no other inhabitants, he is shocked—he would doubtless disown me, did he not think I had lost my senses. Singular man ! How entirely he has lived for his art ! He insists on my devoting several hours to practice daily.

I paid a farewell visit yesterday to *ma chère amie*, Mademoiselle Mars, whose charming society is always so attractive. What a loss to the world is her coming retirement ! how irrepa-rable ! Well may the elegant com-edy of the old school droop its head and sigh over her *retreat*. The fre-quenters of the Théâtre Français will long remember the music of her clear, sweet voice, the chaste expression of her acting, and that faultless elegance of manner that invested every charac-ter she assumed with such incompara-ble refinement, grace and distinction. Molière dies a second time with her withdrawal, and who will pretend to her classic mantle ? In private life the same winning simplicity exerts its spell upon all who approach her. Her conversation is gifted and her amiabil-ity unbounded. How unfortunate the sequel to her career ! Once the mis-tress of a splendid mansion and abund-ant wealth, she is now obliged to econ-omise such resources as her immoder-ate thirst for stock-gambling has left her. Who could associate the spright-ly, elegant Mars with the vulgar ex-citement of La Bourse ? How insa-tiable is the craving after excitement in the human heart, and I think we *ar-tistes* are its readiest prey. * * *

I was at a charming party last night at my dear English friend's Mrs. G. might call her my romantic friend,

for such is the interest she takes in me. I was surprised and delighted to meet some most distinguished and interest-ing persons. One of the king's lead-ing ministers, *the* celebrated Monsieur C——, was there, and attracted no small share of my attention. For a man occupied as he is, with serious, learned and important pursuits, I ex-pected a corresponding gravity and much pretension, and not the levity, witty *homme de salon* he really is. In all other countries such a man would deem it derogatory to his dignity to mingle with the company, sharing in the frivolous chat of such occasions ; but a Frenchman adapts himself, with charming ease, to whatever position he finds himself in ; and, if he fell among savages, he would put on their beads and *paint* with the same nonchalence that he wears a *costume de bal masqué*. The travelled statesman, De Tocque-ville, was among the guests, a dignified person, but rather English in manner ; his lovely wife is as amiable as she is beautiful. The grand-daughter of Lafayette charmed me with her af-fability. What intelligence in her fine eyes !

The distinguished advocate, Charles Ledru, seems a person of great energy and high talent. I have heard much of his eloquence, but poor I have little time for such *divertisements*. I drove home full of gratitude to dear Mrs. G—— for having added to my list such delightful acquaintances, though I spent half the evening talking with her. I find an inexhaustible charm in her conversation ; the earnestness of true feeling robed in such fine expres-sion, and elevated by a mind of such a rare order. She urges me strongly to go on with my Transatlantic project, and aids me heartily in it. Ah ! dear me, how rapidly the days roll on, and soon Paris—bewitching Paris, will be among the things " *that have been.*" Good night.

LETTER IV.

MANAGERIAL POLITENESS—KNAVERY IN AMERICA—MR. WELLES, THE BANKER—AN AMERI-
CAN DIPLOMATIST—BARON ROTHSCHILD—GENERAL CASS, THE AMERICAN MINISTER—AN
EXCELLENT JOKE.

FEBRUARY, 1841.

You are dying to know the result you say, my dear Mina. Well, I go —at least I think so. My mind is in such a pendulous state, vibrating between indecision and uncertainty, impediments and facilities, that I begin to grow curious myself to know the end ; but news has reached me from America. Mr. Price writes, with a gallantry that has quite won me, to name my own conditions, and to arrange it all as I will, but only to come. If this be a specimen of managerial politeness among "the heathen" I hear so daily railed at, chiefly because I persist in going to them, why I have nothing to fear from want of courtesy. I am positively assured by those who have been there, that I shall never be paid, take what precaution I may ; that my dressing-room will be regularly robbed ; that there is no safety in the hotels, nor redress in the law, nor justice in the land ; that I shall be hissed if I dare shew my legs ; and that my private life will be invaded and violated by a press that transcends in scurrility and lawlessness all example or description. These are a few of the good-natured things I hear so frequently, and, if I could believe them, it would be madness to face such perils and such horrors ; but I am incredulous, and curious still.

I have again had the good fortune to make another most desirable acquaintance, the distinguished American banker, Mr. Welles, for many years a resident here, and whose splendid house is the scene of so much elegant festivity and the resort of the first people of Paris. Learning my intention to visit his country (for every body here talks of my monomania), he generously offered to come and give me some hints that could not fail to be useful, and, of course, most welcome. His appearance and manners have quite taken my fancy. Short of stature, with large features, but expressive, mixed with a shrewdness that proves his familiarity with the world. Good nature predominates in his face, and explains the honest and flattering interest he displays for the success of my trip. His manners are singular ; unpretending even to homeliness, but so brisk and animated. Under the impetus of his active mind, he is never still a moment, but with his hands behind him, is running up and down the room, talking as fast as he walks, and saying the most sensible and appropriate things all the time. My *directeur* has much the same habit ; I suppose people with a great deal to think about find it hard to sit still, but when they meet, as happened the other day, I had lively apprehensions I should get run down between them. I took refuge behind the sofa, and enjoyed my security and their conversation with greater *goût*.

Mr. W—— has given me much valuable information, offered me numerous letters, and crowned all by inviting me to dinner, where I shall meet several of his influential countrymen. Really these Americans seem in earnest in all they do, and make you believe in all they say ; and that one never thinks of doing in Paris. One grows sceptical of much even of what one sees among these thoughtless French. I am alarmed at times lest my German frame-work of mind, feeling, and honest faith, should give way under the playful raillery that besets me on every side, and leave me as doubting as themselves.

I have received, all the way from Sweden, a batch of letters for New York, and from a person already alluded to, Mr. C. H——, an American diplomatist. He is certainly one of the most agreeable and entertaining persons I know. He is equally remarkable for his exuberant spirits, his conversational powers, and his varied acquaintances, comprising all countries, creeds, colors, and characters: he is the life of all company, the idol of his friends, the most brilliant of talkers, and one of the worthiest of men; and he must be as well known and respected at home as he is esteemed and courted abroad. He has sent me upwards of a dozen letters to all the great men of his country. If they all come to one of my benefits, I shall not envy Talma his pit full of kings. How grateful I am to Mr. C. H——.

Baron R——d has kindly contributed to my stock, and the American minister, General C——, who has never seen me off the stage, has contributed his quota. I believe the Americans are going to make a sort of national thing of my professional career there. I cannot wonder that they should be piqued by the supercilious remarks they hear on all sides relative to the subject of my going to *their* country. The best-natured people here declare they can never appreciate my art, that it belongs necessarily to a refined and luxurious state of society, and that it requires taste and a large class of pleasure-seeking, money-spending people, to enjoy and recompense a popular *danseuse;* that I can never expect to find in a country hardly yet cut out of its primeval forests, where life is spent in unremitting toil for its necessaries, where few enjoy its comforts,

and where none care for its luxuries, that success which has crowned my efforts in the old world. But different accounts reach me from other sources in which I can rely, and I am led to hope better things. The Americans I have seen with my own good eyes, the treatment I have already received from them, tend considerably to raise my spirits, and I will acknowledge that I am possessed by a deep, ardent, unconquerable desire to behold their far-off land, with its strange people, of whom I hear so much abuse. Come weal, come wo, I declare, with the spirit of an opposed woman, I *will* go; so get your tears ready, dearest, for you will have occasion to shed them, if the loss of so worthless a thing as I am can move you to such an extremity. *   *   *   *   *

I have an excellent joke to tell you of K——, who is, you know, in the main, a very quiet, sedate person, and whose greatest delight, I really believe, is to follow me about, to see I get into no mischief; and though I don't like *surveillance* or observation, as I believe myself fully capable of taking care of my well-behaved self, (am I not so?) yet I cannot find it in my heart to be vexed with her. She has been my very shadow since we were seven years of age together; and I don't think I have gone to a rehearsal or executed a *pas*, or put on a toilette, that she has not superintended. Fortunately for me, in all matters of dress, her taste is exquisite, her invention boundless, and her execution neat and rapid; and to do her justice, she looks upon any toil for me as positive pleasure; and such is her punctuality, that in spite of the interruptions that my vigilant duenna must experience, she has never been too late for a representation, no matter what mighty preparations she had to make for it. She has certainly made herself so useful and indispensable, that I shall never be able to do without her. She does anything but dance for me, and I would like her to relieve me of that sometimes. But now for the joke.

You must know that K—— likes well enough to relieve the monotonous routine of her arduous duties with a little frolic 'when chance favors her; and an occasion occurred lately. You know, at this lively epoch, all Paris is turned into a ball-room, and masques and revels are high in the ascendant. For myself, I get so much of this sort of thing in the way of business, that I consider it a treat to escape such distractions. I never saw but one masked ball, and that offended me in so many respects, while I admit that it was the gayest thing my eye ever dwelt upon, that I never desired to see another. K——, however, must needs go to one of these masked balls; and an acquaintance of mine, Mademoiselle de ——, was to accompany her, to be enlightened, under her sage guardian, in all the mysteries of a Grand Opera ball. It was a wild scheme, for neither of them had ever been in such a scene before, and I opposed their going without escort and protection; but they seemed bent on a bit of nice fun, independent of all masculine interference; indeed, their scheme was to be kept a profound secret, and the preparations were duly made in a most clandestine and confidential manner. K—— astonished me by a flight of fancy uncommon in her; she declared she would go in no other way but as my double. She insisted upon wearing the Cracovian costume. I objected seriously, pointing out all the probable inconveniences that might be expected to occur; thst she would be followed about, talked to, and tormented in endless ways, that a more sober disguise would save her from; and then I was annoyed at the possibility of it being supposed that I had volunteered in such an indecorous folly, so little consonant to my tastes and habits. But she denied the probability of the latter, as the costume was often worn by aspiring gipsies, who left me, however, the monopoly of the dance, and therefore it was ridiculous to spoil the frolic by such idle objections. "*Bien, ma chère*, if you *will* risk it, *comme tu voudrais;* but I repeat my warning, and I have my misgivings of the result."

With the thoughtless glee of a child, she dressed herself *à la Cracovienne;* red boots, blue skirt, white jacket, and velvet cap. There she stood, arrayed in all the panoply of the capering Bohemian. Mdlle. de —— determined upon a black domino; and thus accoutred, they started off in the highest spirits, bent on the brilliant adventures that they promised to detail to me next day; for I insisted on the sanctity of my slumbers being respected, and I left them to their waywardness. My carriage set them safely down *à l'Opera,* and they soon found themselves threading its labyrinths, thronged to suffocation almost, by its merry mobs of blithesome revellers. The masqued "Cracovienne" assailed her numerous acquaintances, and perplexed their lives out of them; right and left she distributed her lively *raillerie.* She had the audacity to attack M. le Directeur himself, and astounded him by her intimate and complete knowledge of all the secrets of the prison-house. She enlarged upon his managerial tactics, spoke of forthcoming novelties, and commented freely upon matters and things in general, appertaining to himself. But, thoughtless creature! she paid dearly for her indiscretion. M. Duponchell declared she could be no other than Mdlle. Fanny; and he said what made him quite sure was, the little feather in the cap was fastened in by a pin he knew I wore.

The game was up, and the news soon spread; the curious crowd rapidly gathered; and as, probably, it was the first time that some hundreds had ever met the supposed one, they thought it a good occasion to exchange a remark or two, with all the innocent freedom that a masque ball sanctions. Poor fated K——! she was overwhelmed by an inundation of enthusiastic admiration; and, go where she would, they followed in her wake, and beset her on every side. At length, teased, indignant, and enraged, she prepared to quit the gay scene of her mystifying triumphs.

But another and most unexpected attack awaited her; she was suddenly accosted by a pink domino, who in good round terms told her she was no better than an arrant thief, to come as she had done that very day, and swindle her out of the costume she then had on; that she did not choose to waste words on such a baggage; and that she must either take off instanter the costume, or pay for it, else she would hand her to the police. The astounded K—— was for a moment naturally bewildered; but conceiving it, of course, a novel conceit of some of her previous victims to pay her off in wordy exchanges, she directed the woman to go away, and turned off to escape the throng collecting about her; but her arm was seized with a good firm gripe, and her assailant, who appeared in downright earnest, told her there was no alternative but to strip or to pay. K——, who is an arrant coward when once her fears are awakened, now began to expostulate, remonstrate, and declaim, but all to no purpose. There stood her adversary, boldly confronting her, one hand holding tight K——'s arm, the other brandished high in air, and flying about with a vehemence both French and frantic. K—— saw all argument was vain; and if she had had the elequence of a Berryer, she was too much frightened to give utterance to it.

So she took the course that it would be wise if all women did when they get into dilemmas—to run for it. She scampered as though for her life across the vast area of the opera house, down the grand flight, spreading havoc among the gay flower-pots, and out into the cold streets; but her relentless pursuer followed her close, and pressed hard upon her, aided at last by the imposing arm of the law in the shape of a policeman. Away they went, helter-skelter, till K—— shot into the *porte-cochère* of her own house, and left the hounds at bay. She came flying breathless into my bedroom, at three in the morning, her hair dishevelled, and her eyes looking wild. This little event has led to all sorts of speculations, and my declaring positively that I was not the heroine of this droll *vaudeville* has only thickened the general confusion.

As for K——, she is particularly susceptible on the subject, and has entreated us all to observe the strictest secrecy, and can endure no jesting about it. I think her next appearance at a masked ball will be indefinitely deferred, and that she will be disposed rather to put costumes on me than incur the dangerous notoriety of wearing them herself.

LETTER V.

An American Dinner—The Lady Hostess—Her Spirit and Manners—Lady Byron—
Elegant Bearing of Americans—After Dinner—The Marchioness.

MONDAY.

I HAVE delayed this frivolous letter to give you some account of my American dinner at Madam Welles's. Her mansion is admirably situated; built, too, according to the taste of herself and husband; and nothing could be better contrived or more elegantly constructed. On entering, I was ushered into a reception-room of fine dimensions, and richly furnished. I was most cordially welcomed by Madam Welles, whom I then met for the first time. She holds a position that she has retained for many years, both highly distinguished and *renommée* in Parisian *salons*. She is of middle stature, and very erect ; thus giving greater apparent height to her person. Her features are good and expressive ; great intelligence and singular decision of character portray themselves in her face ; and the anecdotes in circulation respecting her, quite sustain these striking indications. She is said to have saved at a most critical moment her enterprising husband from all the horrors of a bankruptcy by her energetic conduct, and her bold, determined efforts in his behalf. She went to the Bank of France, obtained an interview with Comte d'Argout, and by a clear and moving statement of the *temporary* pressure upon her husband's resources, succeeded in getting immediate and ample relief. She then went to London, and had the same success with the Bank of England. These timely loans rescued all from impending ruin.

Certainly such instances of energy and capacity are rare among European ladies of these days. The company was sufficiently numerous, but select. My attention was early caught by an elegant woman, simply attired in black velvet, without ornament of any kind, her beautiful arms finely contrasting in their snowy whiteness, as they gracefully lay upon her dark dress. Her head particularly struck me ; large, perfect in proportion, and most intellectually marked ; her features were in harmony with the rest, extremely fine, and most captivating, from the placid expression they wore ; her blue eyes beamed mildly, but with an intelligence not to be mistaken. Here are intellect and a high spirit commingling ! thought I. Her manner further prepossessed me, calm, most ladylike, and yet commanding.

I listened to her conversation, which confirmed most fully my previous notions of her talents. She expressed herself with the greatest ease and elegance, and in a confident tone, that proved her ability to cope with any subject or antagonist. Who can she be ? I anxiously conjectured, and whispered to this effect to my hostess. She replied by presenting me to Lady Byron. I was a good deal moved at the unexpectedness of this sudden *rencontre* with this, alas ! too celebrated lady. Her history and misfortunes have been too often the theme of public and private comment, for one not to have been acquainted with her, before one had even met her. I need not say how fully and entirely I had sympathised with her, for I think it the rigorous duty of a woman, always to sustain her fellow-women, be their errors or misfortunes what they may. Little, indeed, did this gifted and distinguished person stand in need of my sympathies ; but I felt them as warmly and expressed them as fully, nevertheless. Many versions of her unhappy differences with her famous husband have reached me here. You know my aversion to scandal and scandal-mongers. It was enough for me to know that she had lost a home, the dignity of her position, and even the consolation of her children ; that she was an abandoned wife, a mother bereft, and an unhappy, suffering woman.

I regret, as every true, judicious friend of hers has done, a thousand times, that her proud and injured spirit could not suppress its rebellious mutterings ; that an overburdened sense of wrong, beyond her power of endurance forced her, in a thoughtless time, to avenge herself. But enough of poor, unhappy Lady Byron. I must find some room to notice the rest of the guests at Madam Welles's.

Several American gentlemen were there, whose elegant manners satisfied me, in spite of all calumnies, that there are admirable men out of Europe ; and I have seen enough of all countries to know the truth of the French saying, " *Le gentilhomme est toujours, et partout gentilhomme.*" The dinner was excellent ; great variety of rich courses sumptuously served ; and the wines, I was told by the connoisseurs, were of the finest flavor. Wines I judge always by my nose, as my palate takes no delight in any beverage other than plain, unadulterated water. There may be professional reasons for this sobriety of taste, for the pleasant juice of the grape is in decided antagonism to that firm, iron *aplomb* which it is the especial merit of my art to maintain. Therefore I eschew the exhilarating but disturbing influences of "rosy wine." After dinner we adjourned to an upper suite of rooms, and my admiration, I thought exhausted, was again renewed by the taste and costly beauty of these fine apartments.

My courteous hostess, offering her arm, conducted me through the range of apartments, which is terminated, in the most novel and agreeable manner, by a pretty miniature hothouse, adorned with various tropical plants, and warmed to a southern temperature. I never felt anything more luxurious, cold and wet as it was without, than this soft and balmly air.

I grew fervent and poetical, and had already imagined myself reclining, quite *à la Cléopatre*, under the graceful waving of a plantain-tree, in some delicious clime of the romantic East, when coffee was announced, and we returned to the drawing-rooms. Several new comers had entered in the meantime, and, among others, la Marquise de Las Marismas. Her face was most familiar, stationed, as it constantly is, in her magnificent *loge d'avant-scène de l'Opera*. I found, to my great satisfaction, that it continued to wear the same friendly, good-natured smile bestowed so liberally on my stage-vaulting.

I was glad, indeed, the kindness hitherto bestowed on the *artiste* was not withdrawn from the original ; and, though I hardly expect that I shall ever meet Madame —— again, yet the momentary impression of her amiability that evening will be abiding. I left the elegant mansion of my affable host and hostess with the deepest emotions of pleasure, such as I have rarely experienced.

To me, an acquaintance of yesterday, they displayed a warmth and sincerity of feeling I had no claim to, and can only attribute to a kindly motive of encouragement to undertake a voyage to their far-distant country, which they recommend most heartily, never failing to aid me with good counsel, and every kindness in their power. I am most fortunate in their patronage and support. Adieu.

LETTER VI.

Paris, February, 1840.

Since I wrote you last, my dear Mina, I have received very sad intelligence from New York. The worthy gentleman of whom I spoke so gaily a couple of months back, the American lessee, Mr. Price, is no more ! It is mournfully strange that the letter he wrote, giving me *carte blanche*, and urging my coming so strenuously, was the last he ever penned. He fell ill immediately, and with an obstinacy, that I learn characterized him, refused all medical advice. The third or fourth day from the beginning of the attack he desired to be conducted to the window. Looking out on the cold and wintry streets, he observed, "What a dark and gloomy scene is this!" sighed and sat down in a chair, with his eyes still bent upon the heavy clouds floating above, and in a few minutes more his attendant approached him and found him dead!

This event has depressed me a good deal, for though I knew of course little of the deceased gentleman, yet I had anticipated long and intimate professional relations with him. I expected to commence my theatrical career in America, under his auspices, and I depended much on his great experience and known ability, to carry me safely and successfully through the trying ordeal that awaits me. After my first emotions of painful surprise, I thought naturally what effect this would have on my affairs. I considered myself free again, for my contract was made with him alone. His unfortunate death relieved me then, of all imperative obligation, and I determined almost instantly to abandon going ; for, the nearer I approach this great event of my life, the stronger become my apprehensions, and the deeper my anxiety to retreat from its accomplishment. But I fear this is now quite out of the question.

Letters from the surviving manager and *associe* of the late Mr. P. have reached me, begging me not to disappoint the hopes generally entertained of my coming, and that my refusing to do so would involve him in a serious loss, as other engagements had been neglected, in the certainty of my filling up the time. This decides me to go on ; besides I have made much preparation, and I am aware that the Opera here suspects me of employing this *ruse* for certain motives they attribute to me ; this alone would drive me on. I have been very busy these few days back in getting up my farewell benefit. These are usually grand occasions, and I felt especially solicitous that this parting festivity should not fall short in attraction or numbers to preceding triumphs.

I have been making the tour of all the *celebrites du theâtre*, to ask their useful and flattering support, and it has been granted me with cheerful unanimity. It is customary, perhaps you know, for one artiste to *lend* another his talent on thess occasions, requiring the same service in return when the opportunity may arise. It is for each one to judge for himself whether the exchange be equal or not. There are some who demand payment, and they are right. I have secured, fortunately, the *artistes de l'Opera Italien et du Theatre Français*. Of course I have all the aid the *Academie* can afford, for which they expect a good round return of the receipts.

My programme will carry me much beyond the legal hour of midnight, and I must be resigned to the deduction of the fine. I shall pay it the more readily since its destination is a good one. I will announce you the result. I have had several friendly visits from my worthy *directeur*, M. Duponchel. He seems unnasy and dissatisfied at my going, but is yet unwilling to exercise his undoubted prerogative. He has the right to buy my three months of liberty, but he fears, perhaps it would cost him dear. He conceives I set a high value upon it. What woman does not ? He talks of quitting the direction.

I am not astonished at this, but every *artiste* of the establishment will truly regret it. I think his temper much too docile and mild for a position requiring great firmness and energy of character. In our department his ability is manifest, and most useful. In all matters of ornamental composition, in the invention of costume, the decoration of the scene, and in all the endless variety of decorative detail that falls within his province and duty, his faultless taste pursues its elegant way, breathing beauty and attractiveness upon every object it touches. But this is only one and a subordinate branch of his arduous work, and his task is the more difficult, as he has come after one who performed his part so admirably.

It is doubtful whether the Opera ever flourished more brilliantly, or was ever conducted with such skill and vigor, as during the *régime* of M. Veron. In him was mixed up every element necessary to constitute a successful *directeur*: great literary merit, useful, if not indispensable; the nicest perception of artistic excellence, with the exact knowledge of the means to develope it in the most favorable light; an intimate acquaintance with the public taste, and the skill to shape it to his purpose; a most correct understanding of dramatic effects; the greatest sympathy with his *artistes* (too much neglected by *entrepreneurs*), a quick insight into their characters, and wonderful expertness in availing himself of their weaknesses; consummate tact, irresistible energy, and a strength of will that overpowered all resistance. With such qualifications, backed by untiring industry, and vigilant attention to his duties, it is not wonderful that his operatic reign was singularly prosperous, great in profit and fame to himself, and eminently satisfactory to the public.

I came into the Opera at the close of his career, but in time, fortunately, to benefit by his directorial skill and activity. Hearing of my success in London, he came over to examine into my claims. Satisfied that I was not unworthy transportation to the bright sphere he moved in and controlled, he made very liberal offers for myself and sister, which were accepted, and off we started for Paris.

He determined that my *debut* should not take place immediately, and he employed the interval with the greatest assiduity in kindling a curiosity in the public mind concerning me, which he inflamed to the highest pitch of longing. When he thought them sufficiently aroused, and the moment ripe for the event, he announced it with a flourish of his manegerial trumpet that rung through the srartled ears of all Paris. The night came, and my destiny with it. What my emotions were, it would be a vain attempt to portray; but I felt that the result decided my career, that I should remain a favored and admired plant in this rich and coveted soil, or be nipped in the bud, and fall withered and forgotten, into darkest obscurity.

Everything was most judiciously arranged by the vigilant and sagacious *directeur*, for he knew his interest would be greatly affected by the public decision. A *divertissement* was got up for the occasion, and it was so managed that I did not appear until the public impatience was wound up to an almost intolerable point. It was contrived that I should appear with a close veil over my head and face, and which fell so amply down, as nearly to conceal my person. In this shrouded form I appeared on the stage, near to the lamps, and stood thus for a minute, while a pantomimic colloquy was going on about me.

The house was silent, and almost breathless with expectation; my veil was thrown back, and instantly every opera-glass was levelled at my devoted head. I shrunk under the intensity of the gaze, so fixed and piercing; I fancied I was burning under the ardent stare directed so steadily upon me. As glass after glass was withdrawn, the pent-up feelings of the house found relief in loud murmurs of satisfaction, as I was told, being too anxious to determine the point for myself.

My dancing gave equal pleasure, and as the ballet went on, I rose in public estimation, till at the close I was called for, and received the heartiest tokens of admiration and goodwill, more than I either deserved or expected; yes, far more. My success was, indeed, a prize for me. How much had I not to fear from thd experienced judgment, the refined taste, of the French public, and the surpassing merit of my rivals.

Taglioni was then at the very height

of her renown; the matchless creation, *La Sylphide*, had carried her reputation to the uttermost ends of Europe, and her nightly performances at the Opera were hailed with enthusiastic plaudits by her enraptured admirers; and truly her execution was superb and faultless. Graceful as a swan, she glided majestically across the scene, leaving in her wake mute wonder and delight. No one comprehended her perfection more fully, no one one enjoyed it more heartily, than I did. Is it wonderful, then, that I trembled when I stepped forth, night after night, to contest with her the coveted palm of superiority, and divide with her the spoils of public favor? This rivalry, I dare say painful to both, was kept on for a year or two, when she left the Opera for Russia, where her success only equalled her great merits.

I recollect one curious incident connected with her last benefit at the Grand Opera. She solicited and obtained, after much entreaty, the great favor from Vestris that he would appear on this occasion (for he has abandoned for ever *la scène*) and dance with her a minuet. Every one was moved and interested at this novel announcement; the *artistes* especially were gratified at this unexpected opportunity of doing honor to *le dieu de la danse*, once their model, and still their idol. All went on smoothly enough, when it was whispered that the friends of Taglioni were concerting some extraordinary means to do her honor. It was proposed that Vestris the Great should crown her, with all due formality, *la deese de la danse*.

The excitement and uproar this produced among her jealous compeers may be readily imagined; intrigue set industriously to work, open opposition was not wanting, and the *directeur* was called in and appealed to; but, whatever he thought, he could not directly interfere. The partisans of Taglioni were diligent, zealous, and persevering, and they gained their point. The coronation was finally determined on, and the hopes of all pretenders was thus rudely dashed to the ground. It was arranged that, after the minuet was danced, the whole force of the Opera should form in marching procession, and pass round the stage; Taglioni and Vestris were to occupy the centre position, and as they saluted the public in front, the envied crown was to be placed on her victorious head; thereupon a grand galopade of the *troupe* was to follow; of course neither Vestris nor Taglioni was to share in this extraordinary procession.

The solemnity at length arrived; the minuet was executed in the most perfect manner. Vestris, awakened by this momentary return to the brilliant scene of his ancient glory, exerted himself with triumphant success; the *artistes* regarded him with the keenest interest—the public attention was absorbed; his movement was superb, his grace irresistible, and his execution faultless. Taglioni did her part, of course, as became her. The grand event was now approaching— the procession formed——Vestris, wreath in hand, took his place with Taglioni, all tremulous and eager, on his right. The march began, and these principal personages had just reached the front, Vestris was raising his hand to deposit its coronal gift, when, to their joint horror, the orchestra struck up the inspiring, boisterous, torrent-like gallopade! Down came the whole artistic force of the establishment, with an impetus that carried everything before it; Vestris took to instant flight—Taglioni likewise fled; and the desired, hated coronation was thus prevented in the very act of consummation, and of course abandoned for ever.

Taglioni instituted immediate inquiry into this provoking *contre-temps*. The leader of the orchestra was called for, who apologised for his mistake, but insisted that he received the signal to begin—*who* gave it was never known; whether some wag was bent on spoiling the sport, or whether it was mere accident, was never exactly discovered. There were many who declared it was an adroit manœuvre of Mons. le Directeur to keep peace within his disturbed boundaries, and restore order among his agitated and discontented subjects.

M. Veron retired from the Opera with a large fortune and undiminished fame. To the last he was enterprising, persevering, and successful. He gained largely by his experience in matters of business. He engaged me for a limited period at a certain sum. I demanded, on succeeding, that he would extend the term, which he readily did ; but I discovered afterwards that I should have acted wiser to let the term run out, and ask more for a second one.

But to return to present events. I have to deplore the departure from Paris of my powerful and truly disinterested patron, Mrs. G———. I am indebted to her for numberless civilities and kindnesses, that have laid me under the deepest obligations. The more I have become acquainted with her, the greater has become my attachment, the higher has risen my respect. Hers is a masculine mind, that I can lean upon as a sure and strong prop. Her counsel is good and refreshing to me ; and sorely I stand in need of it, surrounded as I am by dangers and temptations, that make my life a perpetual struggle, and no one really interested in my welfare enough to guide me judiciously, or sustain me firmly and boldly. If I have found, as I think, such a friend at last, I shall regard myself as truly fortunate.

I was driving yesterday through the crowded streets, when I heard my name loudly proclaimed, and on turning round observed some one beckoning me with great vehemence to stop. I did so, and the person came dashing recklessly through mud and water to my carriage door. It was no other than M. Laporte, of Her Majesty's Theatre, London. He came in hot haste, and at the last moment, to engage me to begin his season the commencement of next month. Difficulties presented themselves, but the negotiation was agreed to be carried on next day.

How like Laporte to neglect his most important business to the latest hour, and then with what fiery energy he sets to work to redeem his imprudence ! He is a very clever person, and has, too, that peculiar suavity of manner and warmth of address that make friends of all he approaches. He has various and high qualifications for his position, and, were he more steady in the performance of duties, doubtless his affairs would thrive better. He has been singularly fortunate in his managerial career while at the opera. He derived immense profits from Sontag's success, and is said to have left the Opera for Covent Garden Theatre with a fortune of £30,000, which he entirely lost in the latter speculation. His habits, I have heard, are irregular ; he thinks nothing of passing whole nights in gay carouse, and impairing health in sumptuous living and reckless waste. He is an admirable actor. I have enjoyed some of his performances so highly as to make me regret he did not confine himself altogether to the scene as a performer, and leave to some one of calmer mind and more business-like habits the tedious and complicated details of theatrical management.

LETTER VII.

PLEASURES OF FRIENDSHIP—REPUTATION AND SLANDER—PREPARATIONS FOR AMERICAN CAM-
PAIGN—COUNT WALEWSKI'S NEW PLAY—THEATRICAL AUTHORS—ANECDOTE OF A LEGACY—
OF AN AMERICAN IN PARIS.

MY DEAR MRS. G——. Many thanks, and hearty ones, for your flattering and affectionate remembrances of me. I feared, that on your return to your elegant home you would give yourself entirely up to pursuits and friends far more congenial to your lofty taste, and that your petted protégée would cease any longer to occupy your thoughts, or interest your feelings. These apprehensions are happily put to flight by your charming letter, so full of kind sympathy and good counsel ; I accept gratefully the one, as I hope to profit by the other.

Believe me, that I became quite *triste* after your regretted departure. I had become so much accustomed to your delightful society and sprightly engaging conversation, that the sudden loss of both left quite a void in my time and feelings, that as yet no substitue has adequately filled up. How pleasant it was, of a dry, clear, winter's day, to stroll with you in some deserted part of those lovely gardens of the Tuileries, with its fine statues, half-starting into life ; its sparkling fountains, its commanding terraces, and delightful vistas ; and then listen, as we walked arm-in-arm, to your familiar but beautiful expression of thought, that took me up with them, on their strong pinions, and carried me through unaccustomed regions of reflection, where everything was new, startling, and pleasing ; and then, as we turned, your conversation would take a new channel and descend to me, asking questions of my strange

history, that revealed so true an interest, so refined a curiosity, that I delighted to answer and explain.

How deeply was I gratified, too, at your unrestrained exclamations of wonder and satisfaction at the simplicity and almost monotonous regularity of my life, which has been but a series of theatrical engagements, filled up with very hard work and moderate gains. True, events of marked interest and deep pathos dot it here and there, but the canvass of my artistic life is covered over with constant annoyances and petty details. It seemed stale and insipid enough to me, but yet you found in it food for curious comment and romantic reflection, giving it some charm in my eye it never had before. Your candid, honest frankness acted like a spell upon me.

My nature warmed again in the soft sunshine of those enkindling sentiments you so glowingly expressed, and the early openness and *naïvete* of my disposition became again evident ; the reserve and cold caution I am obliged to wear as an armor against the intruding, assailing selfishness of the world, I dared to throw aside in your presence, and to sport and play in all the innocent freedom of thought and expression that is to me as sweet as it is rare and novel. I loved to hear you talk of my past, of "the triumphs and trials of my meteoric existence," as it sparkled in your eye. Familiarity and repetition have robbed it of nearly all its interest in my dull view.

You have often expressed your

amazement and anger at the heavy load of injury which scandal, malignant and persevering, has heaped on my name. Your heart has beat high with indignation as facts have falsified the calumnies that have made my home, cast where it might be, their hideous resting place; and then, to my follies how just, how indulgent you have been! Your words of comfort are still ringing in my ears, "Each of us must shoulder the fardel of her sins, hoping she may make a tolerable 'set off' of virtues and expiatory sacrifices." Yes, I feel, *chère amie*, that my acquaintance with you will give a new and more pleasing aspect to my life; its feverish excitement will be replaced by soberer joys, and, if less romantic, it will be at least more rational.

I have little news to send you. The greater part of my time is consumed now in completing my preparations for my American campaign that you have encouraged me to look forward to with such sanguine hopes. Heaven grant that all your good wishes may be realised! Have you heard of the event of the week, the production of the Count Walewski's play, *L'Ecole du Monde?* For weeks back, expectation has been greatly excited by the rumors that have reached the public ear through a hundred channels, of what might be expected from this brilliant comedy. Little did any one anticipate that all would end so tragically. The prestige that surrounds, like a halo, its noble author, contributed a good deal to the curiosity that prevailed. His imperial descent, his various accomplishments, graces of person, set off by manners the most pleasing and dignified, have made him the lion and the pet of salons and boudoirs, even in Paris, where competition for notoriety and favor runs so high.

In a luckless hour, doubtless to relieve the *ennui* of fashionable dissipation, he betook himself to writing a play for the Theatre Français. This threw all coteries, literary and titled, into a ferment of anxiety and expectation. The committee of the "Français" cheerfully accepted the drama, and every rehearsal confirmed the good opinions entertained. The eventful night of representation came, big with the destiny of play and author. The theatre shone resplendent with the bright eyes of many a high ranked dame, sparkling with delightful anticipation. All ranks and coteries sent forth its choicest representations to do honor to this solemnity—wit, talent, fame, beauty, distinction, and *haute* position, were labelled, broad and clearly, on almost every spectator of the thick throng, that lined the *loges*, covered the *parterre*, and filled every corner of the building. It was a sight and a compliment to make any author proud—an ovation that would have flattered Molière.

But what a catastrophe! The curtain rose, the play went on, the performers exerted themselves to the utmost, the sprightly group was never more alert and gay; but scene followed scene, and fainter and fainter became the hopes of friends, keener and deeper the satisfaction of rivals; act succeeded act, till the *denouement* overtook both play and author. The fate of both was no longer doubtful; and the chilly, funereal silence that prevailed, expressed it all too significantly.

Yes, the poor, dramatic bantling, the first-born of its noble and clever parent, drew but a few short, convulsive breaths, and expired; but if anything could soften so bitter a dispensation, it might have been found in the pomp and circumstance that presided over its interment. I cannot express to you my sincere disappointment and regret at this unlooked-for result, for every one admits and admires the extreme cleverness of Walewski. How he could have failed with such a subject, after such opportunity and with such ability, is the wonder that sets speculation all afloat. His play has certainly various and great merits—it has all the materials of success: composition well chosen and duly combined, much literary beauty, but yet it lacks the essence to give it popular favor— it wants the vitality to make it breathe and move, enlisting your sympathies, and opening up the sealed fountains of the heart.

What is the mystery that makes the writing a good play so difficult? Why is it that minds that vanquish all else, spend their force in vain on this common, but dangerous field? What are the means, where is hidden the recipe, for dramatic success? I know M. Scribe well enough to have extracted this secret, that is almost exclusively his, for failure with this Nestor of dramatists would be as marvellous as complete success with his less fortunate compeers. To others, however, whom it more concerns, will I leave the task of exploring this dark and intricate subject.

I will content myself with merely this remark, that theatrical authors owe far more to their practical actors, the *artistes*, than is either known or acknowledged. Within my own province of ballet, I may be allowed to speak; and if the strangely-fashioned and ill-constructed things that authors bring you for acceptance were put on the stage, with all their imperfections on their head, many a name's bright renown would be damned by failure the most complete and mortifying. Indeed, there is hardly an instance where the ballet produced bears even a family resemblance to the one presented; and it is in no way different with other dramatic compositions of a more pretending order.

I have heard, well authenticated, many curious anecdotes I forbear repeating, concerning some of the proudest names of contemporary literature, to what a ludicrous degree they are indebted for popular favor to the wit and genius of obscure or utterly unknown writers, who are happy in the adoption of their works by some high-sounding name in vogue. In England it is not otherwise. I was lately informed that a celebrated play, *The School for Scandal*, attributed to one of your distinguished authors, Sheridan, was, in fact, not his; that it was sent to him for examination, while manager, and that seeing its great merit, he contrived to retain it for months, till he declared it lost. The title of it was his own, and perhaps some alterations. Truly Fame is an accident, and most rarely wears its own chaplet.   *   *   *   *

I find it impossible to continue my letter, so often am I called away by interruptions that hunt me thickly; visitors roll in upon me in one unceasing tide. Adieu, *et bon voyage*, ring in my ears all day long, so little recollection have I of the kindly voices that pronounce these parting benedictions. A countryman of yours was presented to me to-day by a mutual friend, Colonel W——e; very prepossessing in his exterior, and of fine address. He has an unmistakable air of *bon ton*, and has evidently lived in your best circles. He spoke kindly, or condescendingly, of America, where some distant branches of his family are residing. He has clearly a very indistinct notion of their whereabouts, and I am pretty sure he will never venture on a personal inquiry after it or them. It is amusing to listen to the undisguised expressions of horror of all my fashionable acquaintance at my romantic project. It is not that they are incapable of some curiosity to see what may be seen in the New World, but to traverse it would be, to most of them, worse than condemnation to solitary imprisonment on land.

A ludicrous story was circulated a short time since of M. d'A——, who received a handsome legacy from a West India relative. This flattering mark of good feeling threw him into transports of very sincere gratitude, but it so happened that it was necessary, to get possession of the coveted doubloons, to go after them. Every ingenious means in the world were employed to escape this heavy penalty and charm the distant treasure to his longing *bourse*; but neither law nor magic could aid him, and at length.

he desperately resolved to go. Preparations were made with all possible solemnity, at the bidding, in fact, a final adieu to the world. And who leaves Paris without some such sensation? His will was made, and his friends parted from him with the funeral aspect of a man going he knew not where. He reached Havre, and found himself aboard. The ship was getting under weigh, when his face underwent a mortal change, and, with the desperation of one bereft, he insisted on landing. "Je renonce mon argent, et je renonce mon voyage," he cried. Once more on shore, he turned a complacent look on ship and sea, and then averted his eyes for ever, quietly declaring, "Qu'il aimait bien les poissons, mais pas assez d'être mangé par eux." This is the most practical illustration of the feeling here as to such a voyage. I have some misgivings lest I shall beat a similar ignominous retreat. My places are taken, and my name will go if not its owner. I learn that a distinguished leader of our *haut ton*, la Comtesse de Merlin, will be a fellow-passenger. This encourages me.

I have still another example in an American lady, a Mad. Moulton, living for some time back in Paris in much splendor. Her *salons* have been a good deal frequented, for the French, like other people, have a sharp instinct for a fine house and good cheer. Who hoists a hospitable banner of this kind is not long without an army of hungry adherents. The Americans seem a truly generous people. I hear they give their days to the accumulation of money, but it appears their nights are devoted to its liberal expenditure. Some of the finest fêtes of Paris are under American auspices, for they ambitiously rival, in princely display, some of our grandest siegneurs.

Tout le monde is talking now of a sumptuous festival at an American grandee's, Colonel Thorn, whose brilliant equipages are the admiration of Paris. He occupied a spacious man-

sion belonging to Madame Adelaide, which he fitted up with fairy magnificence and perfect taste. It seems odd, that a simple foreigner, without the prestige of rank or family, should have achieved a position so firm and elevated as Monsieur Thorn is admitted to enjoy. His glittering *salons* are the favorite resort of the most distinguished of title and position in Paris. I do not know by what conjuring he has arrived at such a consummation; but he must have merit, tact, and wealth, in large proportions, to be able to retain it so successfully. His equipages, stud, and servants, are quite upon a royal scale; and, in spite of calumnious insinuations to the contrary, there must be some money left in America to sustain such an outlay. It seems he is a good deal railed at by some of his inconsiderate countrymen, who think, as he is so well able to entertain them, that it is very improper he does not.

The malcontents quite overlook the conventional usages of polite society, and forget that persons must have some claim on the hospitality of another before they can indulge in vague accusations of indifference or neglect. I have heard directly from the colonel's friends, that he is most attentive and courteous to all who come sufficiently authenticated, but that he reserves the harmless privilege of excluding those he does not know, and who have no further title to civilities than the common one of a common country. A number of droll anecdotes have circulated through Paris on this subject, and I listen greedily to anything American, and it may help to enlighten me, when it is so desirable I should be well informed of the character of this marked and peculiar people.

I remember being greatly entertained at a diverting story of some untaught American, who, finding himself in Paris, and left entirely to his own resources for amusement, bethought himself of his far-famed countryman, Colonel O——, and determined on paying him a friendly visit. It so fell out, that on the evening selected the colonel was entertaining at a grand *dîner de cérémonie*, the *corps diplomatique ;* and at the time the unknown guest arrived, attired, most unceremoniously, in an antique frock-coat and muddy boots, the dinner was still going on. He passed the wondering domestics by a quiet declaration of his friendly object of seeing the colonel, and entering one of the numerous *salons*, proceeded leisurely to inspect the furniture, books, prints, &c., and at last seated himself comfortably before the fire, with his feet planted securely against the rich marble mantel-piece.

The great doors of the *salle-à-manger*, which happened to be shut, were suddenly thrown open, and the distinguished company were thrown into a state of dismay which baffled description ; but the easy *nonchalance* of the intruder was adequate to the emergency ; and after taking a long-drawn stare at the ribands and stars that saluted his curious eyes, he rose, in the most cheerful spirit, to shake hands with the colonel, who, by this time, had made his way to the undistinguished object of all this sensation. He explained, in a few words, that he had heard folks talk a deal of the colonel's fine house, and the very pretty things in it, and so he had come to take a look, and he was highly gratified with everything he saw. This was a critical moment for our hero ; but the astonished host displayed great judgment and good feeling in telling him, familiarly, to make himself at home, which he declared, very truly, he had done already.

The matter was explained to the puzzled company, and caused great amusement from its singularity. The " unbidden one " became quite the lion of the *soiree ;* and in going away —which he did at last—he assured his good-natured entertainer, that he was so highly pleased with so many agreeable attentions, that he would do them the favor of his company frequently during his stay in Paris, and it was not his fault that he did not.

You wonder, in the midst of hurry and bustle, I can find time to write you so lengthily ; but I love to renew intercourse with you, even in this unsatisfactory way. Next week I hope to salute you. Till then, adieu.

LETTER VIII.

JOURNEY FROM PARIS TO LONDON—HER MAJESTY'S THEATRE—THE ENGLISH CHARACTER—OPERAS PERFORMED.

LONDON, March, 1840.

Ma chère Thérèse—Such a run as I had of it from Paris to London, from opera to opera, last week, was quicker work than any travelling part of my life of vagabondage that I can remember. Away we went from the moment I waved you my last adieu, rattling, chattering, and splashing over rough causeways and muddy roads, the rain beating hard against the windows of my *calèche,* and the wind sharply whistling around us, till, with a loud cracking of whip, we entered, at eleven o'clock at night, the quiet town of Boulogne.

The packet left at midnight, and we had hardly time to stretch our wearied limbs before we were summoned aboard, and, committing to the careful keeping of my landlord, the truest and most comfortable of carriages, that I part from as an old friend, bound to me by a thousand agreeable associations, I descended into the confined and odorous cabin of the uneasy steamer, whose rolling gave token of the boisterous weather that awaited us, and I gave myself up to sea-sickness and every concomitant horror.

I reached my lodgings near Belgrave Square late on Friday, rehearsed, yet half-asleep, on Saturday morning, and made my *rentree* before my old friends, the English public, the same evening. I did not distinctly feel that I had exchanged capital and people, till my eye wandered, wonderingly, over the dim and vast area of Her Majesty's Theatre.

The contrast of this cheerless expanse, to the sunny and elegant aspect of the French Opera, was striking and chilly enough to wake me up thoroughly to my whereabouts, and, in truth, my first sensations were not the most agreeable. There is something peculiarly repelling in this theatre to the fastidious eye of the continental *artiste*, accustomed to brighter decorations and a more tasteful distribution of the *salle*.

Nothing can be in worse taste than the ornaments so scantily scattered over the house; and then how dull and inelegant is the effect of six tiers of boxes, of extraordinary height, all split up and divided into small compartments, closely resembling pigeon-holes, or, liker still, the cabin-berths of a steam-packet, with their dusky red curtains, that look as if they came off the same piece. It almost gave me a qualm to regard them; 'but, *en revanche*, I have heard the best singer declare that no house was more favorable to the voice, that, notwithstanding its great extent, they filled it with little effort, and that its rebound was most harmonious and agreeable. I received, of course, a cordial reception, for the English are hospitable and kind in their greetings to strangers, and hearty in their welcome to well-remembered favorites, and I feel

it is not presumption in me, at present writing, to class myself in the latter happy category. I like the English greatly; and who does not?

There is solidity and certainty in their character that may be reposed on in friendship, and measured in enmity; nothing shallow, treacherous, or base, disfigures their moral escutcheon. These are noble traits that elevate and dignify the nation they adorn, but the truth must be told, they are likewise very cold, formal, and cautious, even to suspicion, in manner. The higher classes are formidably so in their intercourse with strangers, and very affected in their communication with each other. No offence to my noble patron, I trust.

The middle class is less marked by these forbidding peculiarities; but from top to bottom, through this very stratum of society, run certain dark veins, chiefly of demeanor, that disfigure greatly the natural beauty of their true but latent character. Everywhere in public the conduct of all classes is peculiar, and different from anything I am at all familiar with.

In the Opera House especially, my own sphere, and where I have a right to make my observations, I contemplate them with curiosity. The aristocracy are haughty in their bearing, but they sustain it well in dress and general tenor. Certainly, no where in the world does one see more splendid *toilettes* among the women, or more tasteful dressing among the men—the rich jewels of the former, and the white cravats of the latter, are prominent features, and both effective; but after all, they are not natural, they deport themselves as if conscious the *parterre* was *looking at them*.

While the *parterre*, the people, most respectably represented at 10s. 6d. a-head, how do they act? what is their aspect—their *physiologie*, as the French have it? How different from the free and easy *don't-care-ism* of continental pits; wholly absorbed in the dramatic event before them, and indifferent or unconscious of what their titled neighbors may think or feel. The latter give themselves up to the exhilarating influence of fine music, or the luring seductions of the ballet ; but of the hundreds who fill the benches of the Italian Opera, how few there are who devote themselves to the artists or the scene. How much more of their attention is directed to the stars and ribands of the greater actors who fill the boxes about them.

There are reasons for this ; for, in England, the opportunities are rare, indeed, to see these distinguished personages ; and at the Opera, hours may be agreeably occupied in studying the lineaments of faces that are not more attractive, perhaps, than many on the stage ; but that they happen to belong to people who have made them historical and interesting.

But you are yawning, by this time, over my stage-reflections, so let us to other matters. The *Gipsy* is performing till we can get the *Tarantule* ready ; and how strange it seems to me, Thérèse, not to see you at my side, as ever till this painful moment of our first separation. Need I tell you how heavily your absence afflicts me, and I now discover how much you have lightened my professional labors by your vigilance and attention to endless important details. How I shall get along without you henceforth I know not. Oh, dear ! when I think how the days speed on, and the rapid approach of my now really decided departure, I am half inclined to bolt and turn back again. Don't be astonished if you see me bounce in upon you some *beau matin* next month.

LETTER IX.

LONDON LIFE TO ARTISTS—ATTENTIONS AND PATRONAGE—MEMBERS OF THE PRESS—THEATRICAL CRITICISMS—LA TARANTULE.

LONDON, March, 1840.

I have little to tell you of interest, since my life here is nearly given up to professional occupations. London life to us artists, you know, is dull and wearisome. We come for a month or so, go through our paces, and disappear, without any communication with or knowledge of the people but that we get behind the stage-lamps. Our residence is too short to enable us to make acquaintances, and a foreign language is a bar to improving those we make. The G——s continue their flattering attentions, and bestow on me the most valuable acts of kindness. Such patronage as this is rare good fortune to a poor artist-woman like myself. I have been the undeserving object of much good nature from excellent people in my own country.

The Baroness ——, whom all regarded as the Madame de Staël of Germany, you recollect, took a deep and singular interest in my fortunes ; sympathising with art, she grew fond of me, and lavished many favors where they were well appreciated. But such substantial marks of goodness as I receive from these amiable and distinguished persons are quite new to me, and perplex me the more that they are really so disinterested ; no good on earth can they get by all they do ; *au contraire*, they risk offending many prudish friends ; for, in England, it is not strictly proper to know actresses of any grade, though this would hardly be credited in other parts of Europe. I have met, for the first time here, some members of the press, and a very different class of people are they from those I have lately left ; but I shall not venture on any comparison, for it is an arrogant office to assume the office of critic, and very indiscreet for us, their victims. The one that has prepossessed me the most happens to be a very distinguished member of that influential fraternity. Very judicious ! thank you ; but very accidental, say I, and to be attributed to those winning and amiable manners that make Sir J. E—— a very general favorite. He has treated me with great civility, and his powerful journal has been copious in panegyrics that he declares I really deserve ; and, to tell you my conviction, I don't think I could get them if I did not. Matters are altogether conducted on another system here. *Messieurs les Journalistes* do not frequent the scenes as in *la belle* France ; wherefore, I am puzzled to say, unless this is improper, too, in sober England ; consequently, this high tribunal is not so easily corrupted as elsewhere, where friendly intercourse with the press is more frequent. Believe me, or not, but I assure you that were a rich present sent to a respectable editor here, it would certainly be returned ; while a *" billet de banque "* would be regarded as an insult. The theatrical criticisms in all the English papers are well written, and I think most impartially so. A good actor is praised judiciously, and a bad one condemned mercifully, but it is all done gratuitously. Perhaps no press in the world is more elevated and less venal than all the leading organs of English public opinion ; certainly none are abler or more refined. I regret to have nothing of a livelier character to send you ; but such a life as I lead here affords little incident to comment upon. It is not altogether disagreeable, as you know how absorbing is my love of my art. I am never happier than when occupied with my *" battemens,"* or superintending the amusing details of getting up a ballet, more especially when it is all in harmony with my judgment and liking. I am hard at work with *La Tarantule*, that had so great a success lately in Paris. I have some fear it is not altogether to the English taste— we shall see.

LETTER X.

FEELINGS OF DESPONDENCY—ENGAGEMENT IN AMERICA—THE DUCHESS OF SUTHERLAND— THE OPERA HOUSE.

APRIL, 1840.

This is the last time I shall write to you, my dear Thérèse, ere my departure ; it comes close upon me, and I cannot describe the sinking of heart and the keen apprehension that seize me at times when I contemplate its rapid advance. It is a mere accident that I have not given it up ; but for the, perhaps, judicious resolve of my friends, I should have escaped by the only road possible without breaking an obligation and compromising my honor. Just imagine the director of the New- York theatre writing me a civil letter, stating the financial difficulties of his country to have widened to such a fearful extent, that he dared not prosecute farther a theatrical speculation that might involve him seriously. Had I received this letter, I would have treated it as a godsend, for my courage is clean gone. An agent of the director, M. P——, brought this intelligence to London ; but, meeting a friend of mine, who has all along taken the liveliest interest in my going, and who has sustained me against the most active opposition and endless variety of obstacles, he stated the position of affairs ; but he was urged to take on himself the responsibility of continuing the engagement that his chief had deliberately entered into, though he was told I would consent cheerfully to be relieved from it. This was a dreadful moment, truly. M. P—— saw me at the Opera, and felt satisfied the contract would be—so he politely expressed himself—a very safe one ; but if he should maintain the contract he was ordered to dissolve, the theatre might be closed, and the banner of bankruptcy wave over it on my arrival. The matter was cut short by my friend aforesaid declaring he would assume all risk, and defy all chance of loss, as far as I was concerned, if M. P—— would enter, on the part of his manager, into an agreement for fifteen nights, dividing the receipts of the house without deduction. This was done, and the matter was, of course, referred to me for signature. This was ingeniously contrived, and all my friends joined in advising me to go, if only to save me from the suspicion of having trifled with public expectation for some unworthy purpose. I signed again for the last time ; was ever adventure attended, even from the moment of its conception, with such vicissitudes, mischances, and obstacles, till patience has been a thousand times exhausted ? And yet a strong and steady undercurrent has carried me on, of which I have felt conscious, and yet been utterly incapable of resisting. Next week I leave London, if nothing happens. It would be strange, indeed, if my setting sun in Europe was surrounded by no more clouds.

La Tarantule has met with complete success. This was more than I expected, for the music is made up chiefly of light French airs, that are agreeable in Paris from their comic associations, but they are not equally popular here. I feared the freedom of the second act might possibly offend the conventional delicacy of the English.

The scene, you recollect, is the bed-chamber of Lauretta, when the impatient Omeopatico forces his way, and, thrusting forth the reluctant bridesmaid and attendants, locks the door, and turns upon his victim, who eludes him with endless tricks and stratagems, making the fun of the piece. Nothing can be less offensive in the performance, yet Monsieur le directeur even insisted that the bed should be left out, which destroys the point of the whole act. I made no objection, of course, though I think the public of all countries are made frequently ridiculous in the eyes of strangers, by the aspiring ignorance of persons nowise capable of judging of the true elevation of public taste and feelings. In this case the interference was absurd, for the English, I have observed, are not overstrained in their delicacy, but only fastidious where propriety is at stake.

On Saturday I bid them adieu, and, as always, with sincere regret. From the first I have conceived a strong, deep liking for this noble people—not so extravagant in their phrases of admiration, perhaps, as others, but honest and enduring in their esteem for an artist they have approved. My engagement has been brilliant beyond all expectation. The season before Easter is usually dull and most inattractive at the Opera ; and if the director manages to avoid loss he escapes well, but on this occasion, happily, the attendance has been crowded and fashionable. All parts of this great theatre have been nightly filled, and my spirits, naturally, have been gay and flowing. Her majesty has been present on several occasions, and all the leading nobility. I have been delighted often by the presence of the distinguished lady we have always admired so much, the Duchess of S——d. I have never yet understood the strange fascination this charming person exerts over all who behold her. Whether it is the richness and elegance of her attire, her striking beauty, or the graceful affability of her manners, I know not ; but the spell must needs be strong when it has reached me, who have only seen her from the "footlights." Yes, I quit all with reluctance, save and excepting, which concerns me most, the vilest of all stages.

Never was there anything so ill contrived, inconvenient, and mean ; it runs half way across the pit, as if it had escaped the hands of the carpenter, and gone off on a voyage of discovery for itself, so that a portion of the audience is behind the artists. And then the want of room in the scenes is lamentable, and, at the same time, ludicrous. One goes through such bumping, jerking, and jamming, as almost to dislocate limbs, let alone the tearing and disordering of dresses, and of all things else. They have a custom here of letting in a swarm of sub-scribes, who inundate and occupy the only vacant corners that may exist ; so that getting on the stage is often more arduous than to perform when there. I often find myself in the predicament of an unlucky fish in a glass vase, swimming round and in vain, and find escape nowhere. The dressing-rooms are bad—in short, behind the curtain all is unworthy this favorite resort of the *beau monde*, and the most opulent of European cities. It is to be hoped that some great managerial reformer will one day effect the many desirable improvements there is such evident pressing need of. I must write you a short letter, Thérèse, for time flies me fast, and the great business of "packing up" occupies me to to the exclusion of all else, and I must superintend everything alone. Adieu

LETTER XI.

Departure from London—Grief at parting—Arrival at Bristol.

Bristol, April 14.

There am I, dear ——, almost in sight of the steamer that is to carry me away from all I know and love. I have very much the terrible sensations a poor criminal may be supposed to feel with the rope around his neck, just preparatory to his exit from the state he has been so long accustomed to. Heaven grant that my departmre, in this case, may not be so long a one. I left London yesterday morning, and, amusing to say, we had well-nigh missed the steamer, voyage, America, and all, from the drollest of all causes —everybody over-sleeping themselves. The whole house and servants had been up till three A. M., in busy preparation, and, when the carriage came at eight in the morning, not a soul was stirring. Such a scene ensued of indescribable confusion. The railway departure was at nine o'clock, and we had half an hour's drive to reach it. I limited myself to dressing and rubbing my eyes open, and started with my bonnet in one hand and a bit of bread in the other. N—— displayed that wonderful activity that has so often served in similar emergencies. She came bustling into the carriage at the last moment, upon the top of baskets, parcels, and shawls, in the most ludicrous disorder of attire and appearance. Fortunately, I had no time to indulge the bitter grief that for a moment seized me, as I turned to bid adieu to the dear friend who faithfully followed to the "station ;" but I gave unconstrained vent to my tears for a good hour afterwards, till the fatigues of the preceding days overcame me in sleep. I was occasionally addressed by an enthusiastic friend, who directed my attention to some delicious prospect that glowed in the bright sunshine of an unclouded day in spring-time. Giving now and then a languid look, I relapsed into sleep, dreaming of carolling birds, green hills, and bleating sheep; till at length I awoke in the neighborhood of this bustling, commercial city. After a *nice* dinner, I went to bed at an early hour, to wake upon my last day in Europe—ay, till when? We are requested to go on board the Great Western, of whose splendid qualities and accommodations I have heard so much, at two o'clock.

I will keep this parting letter open *jusqu'au dernier moment.*

LETTER XII.

Embarkation—Fellow Passengers—Accommodations on Board.

GREAT WESTERN STEAMER.

ADIEU, dearest Thérèse. I am drowned in sorrow; and, if it were not for shame, I would fly to town again. You know my rooted apprehension of the sea, that now rises on me almost to terror. I am constantly asking myself, how came I here; it seems impossible I could ever have consented of my own will, and yet there is nothing else that could have done it. We left Bristol in a very small steamer, in which we are piled up together, trunks and passengers, not being able to stir. I had a glance of my fellow-sufferers that are to be; they are of all sorts and sizes, and some look very merry, and some the reverse: class me among the latter. I found myself next to the celebrated Countess of M——n, a distinguished leader of the *haut ton* of Paris, and the well-known friend of all great *artistes.* I had the honor of being presented to her by Mr. W——ff, of the United States, and she gave me a most cordial reception, and tried to cheer my drooping spirits. Madame seems no way dismayed at the dreary voyage before us; but, then, she is going to I felt what was impossible to describe; command favor, while I hardly dare hope to obtain it. As I approach our steam bark, what a mammoth she seemed to the little pigmy vessel that bore us! As my foot touched her great deck, a thrill ran through me. but what a shock I had in going to view my cabin! I had figured to myself something like a good-sized bed-chamber, with tables and chairs (how should I know any better, who was never in such a place before?) but I was ushered into a small closet, as I thought it, and told I was to sleep, and likely to eat. there for some sixteen days to come. I declared that it was out of the question, amid the laughter of all around me; but it is too late now; there I must stay, whether I sleep or not. What noise and confusion! Oh! I hear the creaking of machinery, the sluggish movement of the engine, as if a giant had woke. The steamer trembles as at the danger before it—the wheels begin to turn! Adieu, sister, in tears and sobs, adieu!

LETTER XIII.

Great Western, April 29.

Dear Mina—You demanded of me, when we parted, the earliest details of my voyage. How strange it seems to me to address you now with a vast ocean rolling between us; for I have well-nigh crossed it. They tell me two or three days more must bring us to our destination. This news ought to fill me with singing; but it awakens new fears I never thought of before—a sense of the terrible change that awaits me there, has lately come over me; it is no use to disguise. If I fail, I am inevitably ruined; and my friends in Europe, whom I have disobeyed in leaving them, will join in the laugh and derision that will mock me, and the last two or three days I have spent half the time in vain and bitter reflections; but I am encouraged by the most amiable associations to the contrary, by many of my fellow-passengers. My life at sea has been—could you believe?—quite agreeable, though tormented by vicissitudes of weather, for one does not escape even by going far away from land. Yet the time has passed pleasantly. How cheerfully our voyage began; the weather soft, the sky serene; the sea so bright and smooth, that I thought its glassy surface could never be overspread by anger. Alas! what treachery lurks in its hollow depth! Our days passed gaily: at nine we assembled at breakfast in the immense saloon, some hundred feet long; two great tables running its whole length: a wide space for this repast, with every luxury of earth and sea. Our passengers, numbering 120 odd, were punctual at their posts; and certainly no scene could be more animated: the clatter of plates and hubbub of conversation were new and exciting; and when I listened to it in my cabin, that opened in the saloon, it had a most strange effect. After breakfast, everybody took to the deck; some talked, others walked; and what fine accommodations for promenades! The studious read, and the contemplative mused. I did all by turns, and nothing long. Perhaps the greatest pleasure of all was to lounge in a comfortable chair, and gaze upon the sea, glittering like molten lava in the dazzling effulgence of the noonday sun. I love to think of all the wonders—the "monsters grim" that were hid from my cautious eye by yon sparling mantle that spreads its vast surface over them; and here was I riding swiftly and safely along, like a bold intruder upon the awful element. Hundreds of miles rising up between me and all of those I had never lost sight of before. There was something startling, fearfully so, in the thought; but it did not last long in such merry sunshine.

At three we descended to make our toilette for dinner, that was punctually ready at four. And how plentiful and sumptuous this grand meal of the day; every variety of meats and vegetables cooked in every cunning variety of style: where all came from, or how all was done, I could never see or discern. The attention was excellent, the utmost order prevailed under the vigilant eye of the black steward, George, who, in spite of his short legs and broad back, was everywhere and everything on these occasions; his shining face all covered with perspiration, was a sight—it seemed to reflect its own jetty blackness. After dinner, it was delightful to walk about the deck, and inhale the fresh breezes of the crispy sea, and watch the dying gleams of the sun, whose declining radiance lit up both sky and ocean with its fiery glare—it was beautiful to behold. The evening had its attractions; cards engaged some, and music had its devotees. La Comtesse M——, whose marvellous voice had so often enthralled the gilded salons of luxurious Paris, exerted its witchery here. With an amiability beyond praise, she sang for us, with grace and expression, some of the liveliest airs of her own sunny land, where song and the merry castanet never tire. It was amusing to see the allurement of her music upon the divers groups scattered over the vessel; by degrees, all collected about her, till the covered deck we occupied was thronged to pressure; and the woolly heads of the negroes filled up the doorways, making a dark background to the picture. At the end of four such days as these, it was announced we had made a third of the passage. I began to fear we should get there too soon, this life was so delightful; I went to bed in high spirits. But who can tell the horrors of the succeeding days? the winds blew in hurricanes; the rains descended; the raging sea, lashed to madness, rose as if to engulf us: Tempest, in all its dread majesty, walked abroad. Oh, what a change! and it was as great with me. I laid in my berth, rolling, half unconscious, from side to side, a wretched thing! I saw nothing, heard nothing, but the roaring storm; knew nothing, felt nothing, but such a sensation of—oh dear! it makes me dizzy to think of it. At last I was persuaded up on deck; and what a sight! The wind and sea were still furiously contending. After several days' frightful conflict, our excellent Captain Hoskins, in whose vigilance and skill I felt unbounded reliance, began to get exasperated; and I saw he was disposed to intefere between the combatants. More steam was put on, and the Great Western, obedient to the impulse, rushed into the *mêlée*. Man and the roused elements met; but our course was onward, in spite of the fiercest opposition. Now and then I raised my head, and looked with terror at the mountainous sea that bore us up on its mighty waves, and threatened to hurl us into mid air as we descended rapidly into the yawning chasm that succeeded. I sprung back appalled at the thought of engulfment; but they had an end: " *tout passe, tout casse, tout lasse*," says the proverb, and so did this.

LETTER XIV.

PROSPECT OF LAND—EXCITEMENT—THE LAST DINNER—THE CAPTAIN'S SPEECH—SOUNDINGS.

MAY 2.

We are getting along gloriously; sunshine and storms engage us no more. The Great Western and her noble captain are absorbed in their business, and every day we make an advance of some hundreds of miles. To-morrow we shall see the land they say; how exhilarating the promise! Symptoms of an approach began to shew themselves; the men are shaving off their sea-beards, and the women begin to think of their disordered locks again. The greater part of my voyage has been boisterous and unfavorable. We reached the seventeenth day of an allotted existence, to the annoyance of our esteemed captain, who hoped to put us ashore some days earlier. There was great excitement on board to-day : all the amusements and occupations that have hitherto given zest to my isolated life are forgotten and abandoned in the stirring interest awakened as we rapidly gain upon the New World, whither we are anxiously bound. For myself, I have ceased to think of the adventures or misfortunes that may befal me there ; all other emotions are buried, absorbed, in one deep, intense feeling of curiosity that has taken complete possession of my soul. Oh! how intolerably long an hour sems which interposes between the present and the goal of my boundless impatience. Our last dinner was a joyous one ; and, miraculous to say, after seventeen days eating and drinking of some 120 hungry people, our sea appetites would have made a landsman stare ; the supply seemed more abundant than ever ; the wines circulated freely ; and the eloquence of our ocean orators could no longer contain itself : toasts and speeches succeeded, and the health of Captain Hoskins was drank amid cheers and bravos. He replied with that modesty and correct feeling so characteristic of the man, and bid us adieu with affectionate regret. The confidence I have reposed from the beginning in this admirable commander has never for a moment deserted me ; and his indefatigable attention to his important duties at all hours and in all weathers, has called forth our unanimous and most grateful admiration. No wonder such a man should enjoy such general esteem ; few, indeed, are so entirely worthy of it.

I laid down my pen an hour ago, to run on deck breathless at the news we had arrived on soundings, which simply means that we had passed the bottomless sea, and could, by dropping a heavy piece of lead with a long line, touch the solid earth. That gave me such a sensation as I cannot describe, and it was deepened a thousand times when I recollected that it was *American* earth—that land I had so long and so ardently desired to see. I was standing by as the lead drew up with some of the soil adhering to it. I grasped it with greater eagerness than if it had been a precious pearl, and regarded it with an interest no words can convey. I shall not sleep to-night. How my eyes strain and beam for a sight of this new land ! Columbus, I don't believe, was half so impatient.

LETTER XV.

THE LAND OF LIBERTY—NEW YORK HARBOR—THE BATTERY.

MAY 3, Sunday.

Look there, Mina, behold America ! Since daylight we have seen land, and since that how have I been staring till my sight has grown dim and confused. We have passed the Hook, a point of land around which we turned into a fine stream between two islands, looking almost like a canal, leading straight to the harbor of New York. As we go steaming rapidly along in smooth water, I am every moment enchanted by the lively landscapes that present themselves, so entirely unlike anything I ever saw or fancied. Hill and dale decked in the highest verdure and luxuriating in the richest foliage, succeed in the most pleasing variety. Numberless villas are dotted along the sea-coast, all painted in dazzling white, relieved by green Venetian blinds. These pretty objects are to me so perfectly novel, that I am exclaiming with delight every moment.

The harbor of New York opens upon us. Can anything in nature be more magnificent? Islands of the most picturesque beauty are scattered in every direction the eye wanders to. The city itself is an object of wonderful attraction. A lovely promenade called the Battery, adorned with splendid trees and pretty walks, and running from the water's edge, may be considered its natural frontispiece, and nothing can be more strikingly beautiful to the eye of a stranger.

I have scribbled these lines with my pencil as we steamed along, but my impressions are so rapid and various, that I must give myself up to them entirely. You shall have them, with me, at another time. Adieu.

LETTER XVI.

ARRIVAL IN NEW YORK—DELIGHT—APPEARANCE OF THE HOUSES—THE PARK THEATRE—THE MANAGER—AMERICAN HOTEL.—THE CITY HALL.—BROADWAY—MR. FORREST'S DEBUT.

NEW YORK, May 8.

My dear Madame G——, I send you the welcome intelligence, as you will regard it, of my safe arrival in the western world; and what do I think of it, is the first inquiry you would put to me, were I within the sound of your agreeable voice. I hardly know what reply to make other than that I have been to this moment astonished, amused, and delighted a hundred times with the strange, odd, and beautiful sights that have greeted me at every turn. I arrived on Sunday last, and was greatly struck at first, with the unexpected size and commercial opulence of the city. As we ascended one of the two fine rivers that enclose New York, I observed the quays lined with noble warehouses and fleets of fine vessels riding at anchor in front of them. On the steamer reaching the wharf, I was greatly diverted at the crowd and bustle, and very much flattered, you may be sure, to find that my arrival was making a great sensation, even down to those matter-of-fact creatures, the customhouse officers, who treated all my parcels as sacred property, when I expected just the contrary from the much-talked-of national curiosity. As I drove along the streets to my hotel, I found them singularly quiet and deserted. That I attributed to the character of the day, which is observed here after the fashion of London.

The houses above are of all possible sizes and color, but generally well built and cheerful in aspect; the paving not over smooth, as I felt by the jolting of the carriage, but very clean and nice. On reaching the lower part of the town, my attention was directed to the Park Theatre, where I was engaged. I began to express my admiration of a fine building in marble and of great size, but was soon cured of my illusion by being told that it was the City Hall.

"There is the theatre!" and I looked upon a building as utterly devoid of architectural merits, as any public edifice I ever saw. Nothing could be meaner or more uninviting than its exterior; but I was told not to despair, that my opinion of it would rise on crossing its threshold, and so I hold myself in reserve. I alighted at the American Hotel, where I had been strongly recommended, and was ushered, with great civility, into a handsome saloon, but was promised even a better one on the first vacancy. My exertions had made me quite hungry, so I ordered my dinner, not a little curious to see something of the mystery of an American *cuisine*. I had scarcely done so when the card of my manager, Mr. S——, was brought in. Well, this is prompt and gallant, thought I, and he was shown in; but what a different person from the class I have been accustomed to in Europe, who, dressed in high fashion, display their wit and gallantry in the gayest compliments. Mr. S., on the contrary, attired in plain black, and with a manner most staidly seasoned, had the serious aspect of a man of business. He sat down, looked at me, said the day was fine, to which I cheerfully assented, asked about my voyage, looked again, hemmed, and getting very formally up, said he would call again; and so began and ended, in five minutes, my first interview with an American director. I was told he was rather eccentric, though a very honest, upright man; but that loquacity was a weakness he never indulged in—that he would do anything to oblige you but talk to you. Yet I am sure I shall like Mr. S.

I must confess my first dinner astonished me outright. The table was most elegantly garnished with fine linen and beautiful glass; and—would you believe it?—I was so positively assured by those who had been here that a napkin was not to be found in the country, that I had, consequently, brought some dozen with me. I found them useless. Four or five courses were served, and nothing could have been better cooked or of better quality. There is " science " in the kitchens of the hotels, and I begin to think that America is not quite so barbarous as fine folks have assured me : however, I have some more to see. As I went to bed I put my head out of the window for a look at the stars that twinkled with a brilliancy unknown to me before, but my attention was attracted by the novelties below. The Park lay before me, a pretty promenade, with fine tall trees and well lighted. The City Hall reared its white marble head on the left, and the *façade* of the Park Theatre stood before me in all its ugliness; while to the right an immense pile of gray granite called the Astor House, frowned upon me in the gloom of night. The streets were deserted, though not very late. There was something in the strange objects about me, that told me I was in a foreign land. I gave myself up to meditation, and could have passed half the night at the window; but Katty, ever vigilant of my health, enticed me away, and so ended my first day at New York.

Ever since I have been lost in a turmoil of visits and arrangements. I shall require a couple of weeks to put myself *en train*, after an interval of rest the longest I have ever taken. The excitement to see me on the stage begins to alarm me. The box-office, I am told, is besieged from morning to night, and the mad people are ready to pay anything to get places; perhaps some of them may repent of their bargain.—Managers come pouring in from all quarters, and offers the most tempting are urged upon me : it would be wiser for them to wait and see first. I have been persuaded, almost against my judgment, to give the Cracovienne dance, and the Tarantule, for my *début*, and the dance to precede the ballet. The reasons advanced for this strange overturn of things are plausible enough. The extravagant expectations of my saltatory powers rising so high here, that to meet it is clearly beyond any human effort; so it is thought that my appearance in this popular dance, where the music, dress, and movement are so novel, that criticism will be disarmed, and that the probable effect will be, if not to please, at least to mystify them ; so that whatever disappointment may ensue it will not be fatal, nor cut me off from a chance of recovering all in the ballet. Great difficulty was experienced in getting together a *corps de ballet*, not for want of material, but from timidity to run the risk of criticism. It required great exertions to induce the actors to take part in the ballet, as all shrunk from the really important and arduous part of Omeopatico. At last an old favorite of the establishment, Mr. Fisher, was selected, who promised, from his great comic talent, to acquit himself triumphantly.

I have taken several drives about the city, and have been struck with the width and beauty of many of the streets, and the striking elegance of many of the houses. There are several fine squares after the style of London, and in no wise inferior in extent or effect. The great artery of New York is their favorite " Broadway," of which they are justly proud. It is of nearly even breadth, and runs a distance of some three miles and upwards ; the lower part is mostly appropriated to shops that are well supplied with every variety of fine goods, and tastefully fitted up. The environs of New York abound in the loveliest scenery, which is very accessible by crossing in commodious ferry-boats either of the noble rivers that roll their protecting waters around the city. Who could have imagined that such a city, so richly endowed in natural beauty and monumental sptendor, could have existed in young barbarous America ! We are too much disposed in Europe to indulge the complacent supposition that all that is wonderful and rare in nature and art is concentrated within our borders ; but little do we know of the resources of this beautiful land, upon which Heaven has so prodigally lavished her bounties, and that man has done so much to improve.

I went last night to the Park Theatre, and was agreeably surprised at the neat and elegant appearance of the interior, so strikingly in contrast with its truly contemptible aspect without. It has four tiers of boxes, that are all open in the style of English theatres, with the exception of three private boxes on either side of the second tier. Its proportions are very good, and the ornaments in excellent taste—white and gold. The play was *Macbeth*, for the benefit of a clever actress and great favorite, Miss Cushman. Mr. Charles Kean played the hero of this noble tragedy, and played it well. It is an arduous *rôle*, and demands an amount of physical exertions few actors are adequate to ; but Mr. Charles Kean went through it with great ease and admirable effect, and he made his final exit amid the cordial and unanimous applause of the house.

I have shed my first tears in America, and upon what occasion, think you ? Shortly after my arrival, I attended a performance of Mr. Forrest, the native tragedian, who produced so strong an impression in London a few years ago by his admirable impersonations of Shakspeare. I was struck, on his appearance in a Roman part, by the nobleness of his mien and fine commanding person. He is cast in a giant's mould, and is a fit representative of those classic heroes of antiquity, whose splendid *physique* throws the more effeminate figure of our day into ludicrous contrast. His voice is a most wonderful organ, of the greatest power and rarity of tone ; it rises with the tide of passion, till its loud reverberations fill the very dome with echoes ; and it sinks, in situations of tenderness, into tones of such touching sweetness that no heart can resist. It was to his splendid acting that I paid tearful homage, and never in my life did artist inspire me with deeper admiration.

Mr. Forrest has ardently studied and pondered over the mysteries of his most difficult art. A more refined and accomplished artist I have never seen, and he gives a tint so natural and familiar to his lifelike creations, that you are seduced into utter forgetfulness of the actor, being totally absorbed in the fate of the hero he portrays. This is the triumph of genius. But how useless is it to heap barren words of eulogy on such a performer ! It is idle to attempt a description of his classic attitudes, his noble gait, his enunciation, and, above all, of the fine dramatic expression he gives to every passion of the heart, to every working of the mind. America may justly point to her Talma, and ask with honest pride, if he be not worthy the pedestal fame has raised him to, and the laurel leaf that encircles his brow.

The eventful day of my *début* is upon me, to-morrow will be a *souvenir* for the rest of my life. I cannot disguise from myself the importance of the result. If I fail to gratify the unreasonable ideas of my poor skill prevailing here—and how can I hope to do so?—the consequences will be to me most fatal. My career in this country will end ere it has begun, and my return to Europe will be ignominious. Divisions and malice will meet and mock me, and the brilliant position I have left so thoughtlessly, will be for ever beyond my reach. These reflections quite unnerve me, and I am further alarmed at the extraordinary excitement in the theatrical world. The papers are every day full of details, personal and otherwise. concerning me, and if I was not so agitated, I should be flattered. I will write you immediately after the decision of the public voice, and I pray that it may not be ruinous to my hopes.

LETTER XVII.

FAVORABLE RECEPTION—FIRST APPEARANCE AT THE PARK—FRANTIC APPLAUSE.

May 16.

I am satisfied, nay, far more, rejoiced to my inmost heart, by the most unexpected manifestation of popular feeling in my favor; but I will relate to you the history of the night. I was nervous beyond anything I ever experienced before; this was natural, and I have partly explained it already. I did my best to suppress my emotions, for I felt the necessity of calm but earnest effort. My hotel faces the theatre, and before I went to repose, as is my constant habit on a dancing night, I caught, unhappily, a glimpse of the immense concourse that had already assembled in the street some hours before the doors were to open. There was much excitement among them, and I understood the manager was very apprehensive that some disorder would ensue. He was hardly less alarmed than I was, and heartily wished it was "all over," and so did I too. On going to the theatre I had urgent need of the good-natured encouragement given me, for I had well-nigh lost command of myself. I dressed for the Cracovienne, and listened in the silence of my room to the confused sound of murmurs that reached my ear, and indicated the presence of that excited throng, crowded, as I was told to the very roof, whose judgments I was about to challenge. I trembled in every limb with apprehensions I could not control; I had hardly strength to walk upon the stage. The curtain rose, and breathless silence prevailed; the music struck up, and the moment came, and I appeared. The scene that ensued beggars description. The *whole house* rose, and such a shout ascended as stunned my senses, and made me involuntarily recoil. Men waved their hats, and women their handkerchiefs, and all was inexplicable dumb show for several mortal moments. I stood confounded, and tears streaming down my face. Order at length restored, the dance began. How I went through it I know not ; I was scarcely conscious of what I was doing. I felt only one dreadful sensation of a great weight being attached to my limbs ; or as if palsy had stricken them. But I must have danced as I hope never to dance again. I was *encored* to the echo, and in a few moments recommenced amid the most cheering applause. A vaudeville succeeded, and I retired to get ready for the ballet. I was not curious to know the feeling of the house, for I feared it must be unfavorable. I began to warm to my work, and my ambition awoke. I resolved to make some desperate efforts before I yielded the struggle. I soon learned that such a state of feeling prevailed as had been calculated on. Great confusion of opinion and impression, perhaps some disappointment, but just that blank state of mind that I might hope the most from. This roused my soul to action, and I longed to be at them. As I dashed in for the ballet, the sensation was hardly less strong than at first. My appearance in feminine and coquettish attire seemed more in harmony with their expectations, and they evidently liked my looks. A loud murmur of surprise and intense satisfaction rose on every side, and gave me a stirring impetus. It is not for me to say what I did, or how I did it, but never was I carried so resistlessly along on a buoyant tide of feeling that bore me quite away. I danced without effort, aud even Katty applauded some of my feats. The most deafening exclamations of delight broke at rapid intervals from all parts of the house, till they lashed themselves into a perfect tempest of admiration. Never before did I behold so vast an assembly so completely under the sway of *one* dominant feeling, and so entirely abandoned to its inspiration. The curtain fell amid a roar that sounded like the fall of mighty waters, and that soon brought me before them. Their applause was perfectly frantic, cheers and bravos saluted me, and flowers and wreaths fell like rain upon me. You cannot suppose that I stood unmoved amid such sights and scenes. My heart beat till I thought it would leap from its socket, and my eyes overran in grateful testimony of their fervent goodness. I essayed to speak, and stammered forth a few simple words of thanks, and withdrew. The ordeal is past, doubt no more affrights me, and what a prospect dawns upon me ! Heaven grant that the end may prove worthy the auspicious beginning I have just so feebly recorded. Adieu.

LETTER XVIII.

The Clime and People of Havana—Hospitality—Customs—The Theatre—Poetry—Walks and Drives—The Spanish Company—Habits of the People.

Havana, February, 1841

Dear Sis—An opportunity presenting by Don ——'s going to Paris, I write to you what you never have learned through other channels, of my complete success here, that goes on still increasing. The people seem jealous of the *éclat* I acquired in the United States, and are anxious that good report should be made at Paris of the cordial reception they have given to a truant *danseuse*. I have fearful misgivings, at times, that I have lastingly forfeited Parisian favor. I stand in greater need, then, of all the consolation my wonderful career ought to afford me. Notwithstanding your deep disappointment at my non-return to Europe, yet I am persuaded you are gratified at the continued good fortune that follows me, emptying its veriest treasures in my lap with prodigal hands. I am delighted that I have come hither, not for the extension of my *renommée* merely, but rather for the charm I find in everything that surrounds me. The sky, the clime, its luscious plants—the people, their generosity, their hospitality—and scenes and sights that are so novel and pleasing—all combine to make my residence here indescribably pleasant, and will furnish my memory with some of its most brilliant retrospections. You would have been greatly amused last night had you accompanied me to the opera. It was for the benefit of Mdlle. Obee, a very charming person, greatly esteemed here; and popularity is here, above all other places, profitable to an *artiste*. It is the singular custom for the *beneficiare* to sit at the public door of entrance behind a table, supporting some silver dishes, into which are thrown by the comers-in such sums as their generosity prompts them to give. The sound of this is very offensive to us, totally habituated to another method; and this public display of one's self on such an occasion, and for such a purpose, seems quite intolerable. I think I could never support the rude gaze of the crowd, and would shrink from such an ordeal, but how the sight of a thing altars preconceived opinions! Mdlle. Obee sat there, smiling and bowing to her friends as they entered without regarding the gold they deposited, and chatting easily with others, apparently unconscious of any awkwardness or oddity in her position and it appears far less so to me now. The truth is, public attention is more pointedly directed towards those who are expected to display their generosity; to these I am sure the *exposé* must be the most trying, for a hum or murmur of disapprobation or disappointment usually follows any mark of liberality or niggardliness.

I believe this usage is familiar to Havana. I never heard of it elsewhere. There are other features that are equally distinctive. Visits are paid to all your distinguished acquaintances, who are especially invited to the festival; boxes are retained for them, unless they signify their inability to come; tickets are sent, also, to all the influential persons, who retain or return them with excuses; but no charge whatever is made on these occasions. There is a suspension of prices, and all is left to the discretion of the comer; tickets at the usual prices, are sold for those parts of the theatre where the promiscuous part of the audience go, the upper galleries, but for neither the *lunettar*, or boxes; and the eye is therefore rarely offended by the sight of vulgar *silice*. Pieces of gold of various amounts display the quality and munificence of the *artiste's* aristocratic patrons. The currency is quite a treat here, after the dirty and doubtful paper money of the "States." It is all in solid coin of gold and silver, of various sizes and values, fractionizing from the "onsa," or doubloon, (a beautiful coin of very pure gold); into halves, quarters and eighths, also in gold, and easily distinguished. The coin of silver most in use is called "paseta," and is about the value of a franc. I am glad to say I have had opportunities of becoming quite familiar with this useful material, as Don Marté presents himself, per agreement, every morning succeeding the performance, with the said 1000 dollars that were agreed on. The benefits in Havana of the more distinguished *artistes* are profitable, yielding an average of 2500 to 3000 dollars, with very small deduction for expenses. There is another source that enhances the amount, and more agreeable to a fine *artiste* than the pecuniary demonstrations — the "presents" that it is usual to make in private as tokens of friendly esteem. These depend for their value and number, altogether on the popularity of the *artiste*; so there is a constant stimulus to good behavior and amiable deportment, that exercises a favorable influence on the conduct and manners of the *artistes* at the Havana. Mdlle. Obee was very well sustained by her numerous friends ; and besides a golden harvest at the door, she reaped whole fields of flowers and complimentary verses on the stage. It appears there is a great deal of poetic fire among these glowing sons of the tropics ; if such heat did not hatch poets one might despair of the brood in more ungenial climes.

I have great reason to be flattered at the high-flown effusions of torrid poesy of which I am the favored subject in the papers here ; poetic garlands, of bright and varied hue, are daily woven for me. They wreathe my heart from the graceful gardens of their fancy, while they heap on my head the choicest gatherings of their rich and variegated soil. I am hardly well enough acquainted with their pompous, but ardent language, to judge of the merit of the former, but my deep and long love of the latter fills me with delight as I contemplate their endless varieties, and their exquisite beauty. Oh! how I adore flowers! My eyes surfeit on them, and their delicious odors intoxicate my other senses. My fancy is enslaved by their very purity, and musings the most agreeable, reveries the most exhilerating, take possession of me in regarding these emblems of innocence, these emanations of earth's poetry. I like to see a woman fond of flowers, she must have redeeming qualities about her while she can tend and foster them—at least, I must have some theory to defend my avowed love of them, and, certes, I have had a lavish share of them. Would that I had numbered the splendid wreaths alone that have been showered upon me so profusely, the figures would surprise. I have cautiously put aside such of them as are associated with particular occasions, or affecting events, and I guard them with jealous care. Now and then I take them out, and gaze on their withered leaves and faded ribbands, till my eyes fill at the recollection of the enthusiasm that prompted these gentle gifts ! How much l value them, how kindly I shall ever treasure them ! I wish, my dear Thérèse, that you were here, to get with me into one of these grotesque, yet comfortable swinging *volantes*, and take a drive on one of the most charming promenades I have any where seen, hardly excepting the magnificent ramparts of Vienna. But this is totally a different thing. Imagine yourself just without the city walls, moving gently along on the aforesaid *volante* over a smooth road of upwards of a mile in length, planted on either side with double rows of young but thriving trees, adorned with graceful fountains in marble, whose trickling waters fall gratefully on the ears. At one end of the road we are just turning, you see a very noble edifice ; you mistake it for a nobleman's palace. Imposing as is its exterior, it is devoted to darkness and crime within : it is the Taçon Prison. In ascending you observe that this part of the road is but newly opened, and as yet incomplete. A fountain is erecting here, the grounds adjoining are being laid out for ornamental purposes, and there some pretty houses are in process of erection. On reaching the middle part of the promenade we find ourselves opposite the main entrance to the town, with a very striking building of great dimensions rearing its colonade on the right. I look upon that, you see, with a familiar glance of recognition—that is the Taçon Theatre. We pass on and find ourselves in the most beautiful portion of the Paseo. It is six o'clock, the witching hour ; and now that the scorching sun of noonday has passed on his fiery course, casting back the mild radiance of his declining rays, softening the beauty of earth, and shedding a glory upon the southern skies that it is delight to look upon. At this lovely hour behold every city gate pouring forth its daily frequenters of the Paseo ; the walks are crowded by gay pedestrians in sociable converse ; while the stone benches, liberally provided for the loungers, are occupied by others who calmly gaze on the panorama before them, luxuriating in the passionate enjoyment of their *cigaritos*.

On either side of the carriage road is a string of *volantes* moving in opposite directions, of all shapes, colors, and pretensions—the elegantly adorned and silver-embossed harness of the rich noble's " turn-out," to the more unpretending one of the homely cit. It is amusing to see the passion a Havaneco has for a *volante* ; it seems with him the first necessary of life—his *vademecum*, his food and drink, making his life luxurious, and his ambition contented. There is more in this than the mere usage, or as determining his claim to respectable competence ; in truth the climate requires this indispensable *agrèmen.*

You smile incredulously at my complaint of heat, when one should be shivering by *rights* with cold. Here am I—yes, it is February—languishing under the subduing warmth of a temperature at 80° Fahrenheit ; summer insects buzzing in my ears, and choicest fruits slaking my parched mouth. This is certainly a droll revolution of seasons that fills me with daily wonder ; I thought all such magic was confined to the opera house. I used to be puzzled in Paris when told that the Americans were five hours behind us in time, and that we were snugly in bed while they had the evening before them. I fancied then these Americans were a clever people and that they even got more out of Time than the old ones of Europe could contrive. I have never doubted that this was so, having had it on good authority, but I shall never quite believe it till I can prove it for myself, and there is little chance of that before somebody—it will be, I am sure, a Yankee—invents a plan of being in two places at one moment. But there is no deception in this charming improvement of getting up a magnificent

summer in mid-winter. Just look at those ladies in their open *volante*, in full dress, as is the custom of an-afternoon on the Paseo. Low dresses, short sleevs, no bonnets, a graceful mantilla supplies its place, fans in their hands, roses in their hair, fire in their eyes, mischief in their glances, smiling soft recognitions to friends and acquaintances. How could such things be if their *toes* were cold, and a sharp wind was making havoc with their noses ? I tell you the air is balmy, the sky serene as a good woman's conscience, and the warmth languidly oppressive, and it is the 10th day of February, 1841. Now put away your incredulity, Thérèse, and believe that all is not profit in Havana, and that one must travel not merely to dance and get glory, but to see and feel that which can't be seen or felt elsewhere.

On the mid-way between the vehicles are groups of horsemen, who ride badly enough, enlivened by officers in military attire, giving relief and animation to the rest. The horses, for the most part, are sorry jades. Mules are in great requisition for the *volantes*, and are little adapted for the work. The native horse is small, but strong and flat, with enormous chests and flowing tails. Such is the " full dress" of a fashionable horse in these parts. They are pretty-headed, and bright-eyed, and would look well in lithograph. If you have grown tired of the up and down driving of the Paseo, we'll follow the crowd to the Taçon Garden, some very prettily laid-out grounds enclosing the summer residence of the captain governor, a couple of miles from town. My first visit was rather amusing. We had descended from the *volante* for a walk ; a beautiful moonlight night, we sauntered down an *allée*, that looked too inviting to resist ; we pursued it till we found ourselves in a sweet garden, where we wandered wondering and delighted. At every turn a new and agreeable surprise ; a *jet d'eau ;* a gurgling waterfall, with its moss and grottos ; we ascended terraces, sat down in arbors, wound through thick-leaved groves, and while astonished at our presumptuous intrusion, we wondered if it had an owner, as we saw no house, heard no keepers or servants, nor the barking of some vigilant dog : all was silent and enchantingly lovely on the bright moonlight. After wandering around and about till we were tired, I sat down half awed by the mysterious quiet that pervaded everything. I had no idea where we were, whether on public or private property, at what distance from the city, and now we had even lost the way out to our *volantes*. Perhaps, thinks I, we have been decoyed into fairy domain ; and when the leaves fluttered in the evening breeze I looked round for some little elf to summon me before her queen. I thought of the magical gardens in the *Arabian Nights*, and all the droll things and queer tricks practised on the fairy adventurers into those unknown precincts, and I really began to feel quite uneasy ; such is the effect of imagination. I started to find my way out, and had not gone twenty paces before a sudden turn brought us upon a gay group of ladies and gentlemen, who stared at us quite strangely. I passed on as they bowed, and got out at length, to find I had been making so free with the captain-general's gardens. The road that connects these grounds with the Paseo is laid out with great pretension—fine trees, stone benches ; but is fallen into sad condition, and for an odd reason ; it was constructed by George Tacon, who seems to have taken Havana up by the arm and jumped into another century. He has conferred inestimable benefits on the place, adorned it with noble edifices ; embellished it with gardens, squares, and fountains ; gave security to its streets by clearing them of robbers and assassins ; and promoted its health, comfort and convenience in a thousand ways ; and, sad to say, as is too often the case with benefactors, public and private,

hated for his pains. I mean not to reflect on the want of generosity of native character that prevents them acknowledging these great benefits ; but it seems Tacon was disliked for his high-handed energy that impelled him so far as to make him undertake and accomplish whatever seemed useful or good unto him. Query, would he have done any good had he acted differently ? How often a true friend is forced to oblige us against our will ; but noble natures acknowledge the service gratefully, and I am persuaded the Havanecos will yet erect a marble monument to Tacon, who has laid them under such deep obligation.

But here we are back on the Paseo again, and though nine at night, we find the scene still gay ; the walks animated by groups in merry chat, the cigars of the men outshining the sparkling eyes of the fair dames, the incessant rattle of whose coquettish fans gives notice, like the generous rattle-snake of the States, of the danger of approaching within the pale of their fascination. Really it is pleasant thus on a soft, bright night in June—no, February—to loll in a *volante* and be slowly *entraînée* up and down this delightful promenade amid lights, and music, and waterfalls, and lively throngs ; but the drive home again is a great treat. The houses here are droll, fantastic things, certainly ; of all colors, fashions, and sizes ; but most of them seem constructed to gratify the curiosity of strangers, for what with immense windows without sashes or glass, and wider doors, it must be an immense effort of good breeding that prevents you seeing what the family are about within. It is the fashion I observe, to arrange six or eight chairs in the middle of the room near the window, facing each other, when all the company sit with great gravity talking with and gazing at each other. Innumerable groups of this kind one observes on passing. In other houses the family will be grouped round a table ; elsewhere dancing ; often discoursing through iron bars, that protect the windows from I don't know what, with acquaintances standing in the street. This is the case usually between the young unmarried, who are kept apart in this bar-bar-ous way as under better moral restraint. Another oddity is the doorway, or *porte*, between which is almost invariably the coach-house, for here stands the treasure, the idol of the house, the *volante*. And when these great doors open into the principal room of the house the *volante* has the best corner in it. There it is, with its head up and shafts down, with a quiet, complacent look, as though conscious of its value, with the family group around, under levee, and lawfully protected from soil or touch. The stable usually is in the court-yard of the house, one side of which is furnished with a manger and sometimes a covering, for in this delightful clime the latter is not indispensable. This is thus a very close neighborhood, and a disagreeable one on many accounts, between the inmates of the house and the stable. But the natives care nothing for this; the horse, or mule, is as necessary as the *volante*, and both are equally favored. I am speaking now only of the smaller domiciles of homely cots. There are in Havana many mansions of an extent and splendor that would arrest your notice in the first capitals of Europe; the house of the Marquis d'Alcos, of Don Montalos, Counts de Penalvec and de la Recencon, &c., are as striking for their gardens as admirable for their style. But of this another time. You must be tired, Thérèse, after your "drive on the Paseo," that you must fancy you have taken with me, and I will spare you my chatter till another day.

I went on Tuesday to see the Spanish company perform, as they do three times a-week, at the Salon Theatre. There are some good *artistes* among them, imported by the indefatible Don Marté from the mother country. In his managerial lists you find *artistes* of as different qualities and varieties as

you do acquaintances in his real ones. Which he *makes* most of, the object of all his enterprises, I don't know; but which he is most in harmony with, I do know. The play was interesting, and warmer in its action than I expected a Spanish drama to be; they are mostly cold and stiff, and too Castilian in their gravity; but this called forth the passions of the *artistes*, gave scope to the expression of feeling, and was effective, dramatic, and exciting. One real incident of a distressing kind called forth the painful sympathies of the audience. An actress of superior merit, the heroine of the piece, whose acting had greatly engaged, had the misfortune, in the energy of her movements, to overbalance, and she fell with great violence on the stage. She was instantly picked up, and removed. It was soon announced that she had broken her arm in two places, and was unable, of course, to appear again. This damped the audience for awhile; there was a long interval. I was much shocked, and disposed to go away. The farce, however, followed, and I saw evident symptoms that it was greatly relished.

The Havanecos seem to enjoy a farce with hearty good-humor, a real joyous sympathy with its fun that sustains my notions of their deep good nature; every droll incident and diverting turn brought out shouts of merriment; while constant laughter recompensed every witty expression and playful mistake. There was one very old man, who was the marked favorite of the audience. He is said to have lost much of that elastic humor and buoyant facetiousness that made him in years gone by so irresistible; he still preserved his mastery, however—for a single look convulsed the house. I divined at once his charm, or, rather, felt the spell, and saw from whence it emanated; it was in his face—its laughter-moving power, while every muscle stood rigid, its penetrating humor, that sought mirth in its innermost recesses, were, indeed, quite vanquishing; and often, without knowing a word he said, I laughed as heartily as the rest. How mysterious is this gift of true comic humor; how few actors I have ever seen it in all its genuine breadth and richness!

I cannot close my letter without giving you what may interest you most, some account of my theatrical progress here, that you have doubtless heard much of already. I am making great and rapid advances in popular estimation here; and, accustomed as I have been lately to the most boisterous tokens of admiration, there is still something pleasing and exciting in the frantic applause that hails me nightly from this new people. Their complimentary homage has taken a very fanciful flight indeed, but to me a really charming one. As I finished a pirouette last night with singular felicity, imagine my surprise to see lighting at my very feet two beautiful doves, bearing a snowy wreath outvying even their lustrous whiteness. I accepted the offering from my winged messengers, but was so barbarous as to detain them as a lawful prize. I took them up, and carried them away to my dressing-room: the house cared nothing for the interruption; *au contraire*, I found my acknowledgment of the compliment gave them infinite satisfaction. Had I neglected it, they would have been greatly mortified. They like coquetting with an *artiste*, and it is agreeable enough to me to humor them in such a way. It is amusing the interest taken in these playful manifestations of regard; but they serve, I see, as stimulants to enthusiasm, that goes on in a steady, deep current, increasing, till I am puzzled to know where it will end. I am always half startled at such excessive excitement; I tremble lest in a giddy moment I should do something to turn the tide, and when the sea is in such violent agitation a change of wind is certain destruction: may the fairies protect me! Would you were here, Thérèse, to have a peep at the world so peculiarly our own from behind the scenes. What sights and sounds! you

would fancy its inhabitants all painted brown for a gipsy piece; and then, the strange, unintelligible gabble they carry on. But your sense and patience both would be sorely tried, as mine is, by the horrid, suffocating fumes of tobacco. Everybody smokes here— man, woman, boy, and girl, almost down to the baby just escaped from the cradle; but still I was not prepared for the novel spectacle of the very "sylphides" themselves strutting about with huge, undisguised, veritable cigars in their mouths, puffing and smoking like so many yellow chimney-pots, that they resemble much both in symmetry and color. Smoking I detest, as one of the most insufferable and nauseous follies of the day. Strange that men should persist in this offensive habit that all women with pretensions to a nose at all civilized unite in condemning; yet custom has inured men to this. But a woman's smoking was a barbarism I hardly supposed myself destined ever to see; and, certainly, the first time I came plump upon one of my whitybrown attendants, with her wreath on one side, her wings all awry, sucking, for dear life, at the end of a flaming cigar, my astonishment and the tobacco-smoke together quite took my breath away: that was an impression neither time nor distance will either dim or remove. A full-dressed sylphide sitting on a painted bank of flowers, where I first spied her, exhaling the smoke of a colossal cigar, and of a horse-killing strength, with all the *nonchalance* of a veteran smoker, was an outrageous novelty that absorbed me quite; and while I stood gazing there, a call summoned the volcanic *troupe* to the stage, and each one deposited with jealous care her precious weed on bench and chair, with growling menaces neither to touch nor taste, and then they betook themselves to their mystic gambols, meant to charm the love-lorn "Reuben" to their *fairy haunts*. It requires faith in one's art to preserve illusions amid such scenes. Surely *nasillées* are strange things;

and who can hear of such marvels, and believe them true, *sans* exaggeration, *sans* distortion ? I must redeem, however, the *ladies* of Havana from the charge of any proneness to this odious habit ; it is confined to the women of the lower classes. The men of all degrees smoke, and smoke everywhere ; in the houses, in the streets, in the theatres, in the cafés, in the counting-room ; eating, drinking, and truly, I suspect, sleeping, they smoke —smoke—smoke ! It is odd that strangers don't scent Havana far out at sea ; the gentlemen, however, are addicted to a small paper cigar, called " cigarito," containing a small quantity of pulverized tobacco, of the best flavor, which is by no means offensive. No true Havaneco even moves a foot without his portable armory of cigaritos—as indispensable to him as is his quiver to the wild Indian. He may get along comfortably without his coat, hat, or neckcloth ; but without his cigarito he could neither walk, talk, nor even think. The first thing that follows a salutation of friends, meeting no matter where, is to pull out their pacquets, light the sociable weed — another talk : it gives life to the Havaneco, he opens his heart and mouth at the same time, and fills up the gaps of conversation. A cigar ought to be the national emblem of Cuba ; certainly, nothing is more completely identified with them in my mind, and I shall never recall a friend to memory who will not be enveloped in a soft haze of tobacco-smoke.

LETTER XIX.

Journey from Charleston to Havana—Accommodations on Shipb ard—Jolly Captain— Interesting Story—A Solitary Stranger—Storm at Sea—Mail-Packet—An Indian Legend—A Tropic Panorama—The Harbor of Havana—The Hotels—A Volante—Lodgings—A Predicament.

Havana, January, 1842.

Dear Mina—You wonder, and not without reason, at all my odd adventures, amusing good fortune, and strange wanderings, but not more than I do myself. I live and move in an atmosphere so brilliant and stimulating, that I am quite lost and unconscious of the reality of things. My senses are steeped in a sort of eddy of intoxication, till drowning seems inevitable ; but before I am quite gone, let me make one effort to give you some account of my late travels, and that in as sober a manner as I can.

Well, then, I left Charleston on the 3d instant, and committed myself with trembling apprehensions to the queer little boat they called a schooner destined to bring us here. The first sight of it drove me to a declaration that I never would put my foot aboard ; not but that it was pretty and inviting enough in itself, and, for a pleasure-party on a great lake, I should have been delighted ; but to venture out upon the wild ocean that I dread so much, in a vessel no bigger than a fair-sized sea-shell, I shrunk from. At last I was persuaded, because there were no other means.

We got off on Sunday morning ; the sea was calm enough, and little wind ; but ere many hours had elapsed, I had unequivocal indications that there was something wrong within ; and I sought to compromise the matter by lying down and trying to fancy myself any where but where I happened to be. In a day or two my sight became steady enough to gaze calmly about and in a reflective mood, hoping to find distraction in the task. I had not to look far, for in the smallest circumference imaginable I found myself cooped up in a friendly neighborhood with boxes, barrels, pigs, chickens, and fellow-passengers, all mixed in strange confusion together. How very republican in its effects is this prostrating *mal de mer!* how effectually it levels all ranks and distinctions down to a flat equality of sickly indifference to all things sublunary! but, as the visitation passed away, things, people, and poultry fell back into their respective positions and places, and order began to smile on us again. Certainly we stood in need of the convenience that could be gained from the most judicious arrangement of matters, for we were pressed into the scantiest possible limits.

There was a cabin on deck for the gentlemen, and which had double its complement; there was a dark, doubtful-looking place somewhere below, styled "the ladies' cabin;" we had in addition some six feet of deck-room for out-door exercise and air; the rest was variously appropriated to cargo, water casks, live stock, &c.; we had twenty and odd passengers, and not room for half the number.

Just imagine our situation! what a condition for me to come to, that up to that epoch had been rather luxuriously accommodated, and who had certain fixed notions of living totally in contrast with the scene around me. To add to our annoyance the wind turned perversely a-head the third day out; but there was something novel and very comical in all this, and I was amused.

The captain, too, was a perfect fountain of good humor, ever bubbling and overflowing, and full of the wittiest sayings and the liveliest remarks. It was impossible to resist his pleasantry; though pecuniarily a sufferer by the prolongation of our voyage, yet he bore it not only without a murmur, but seemingly enjoyed it. He was a round-faced, broad-shouldered, droll-looking fellow, and the gay tones of his voice communicated sprightliness to all within its exhilarating influence. I thought he never could have said a cross word in his life, much less have done a passionate thing; but one day, with a view to amuse us, he was displaying such curiosities as he had picked up in his wanderings, when I caught up a pretty stick that had been brought out with them. I thought I detected a change of expression in his jolly face as I examined it, and at first he evaded answering inquiries about it.

Being pressed, he said it was associated with one of the most tragic events of his life; and, taking the cane from my hand, he drew from it a glittering blade, and observed that he had been compelled on a sad occasion to run it through an unfortunate man, killing him on the spot. I recoiled from the murderous instrument with horror, and though I received the fullest explanations that self-defence demanded the sacrifice, I could not disassociate the captain from so frightful a deed.

Many foreigners, on hearing such a recital, would come to no very charitable conclusion on the state of society where events of this sort could happen; but while I am influenced by as sincere a feeling of sympathy as any one for a wretched fellow-creature thus rudely cut off, yet I have sense enough to admit that such a catastrophe may occur any where, and the best regulated communities of Europe are outraged by similar deeds. It would be unjust to form a harsh and condemnatory judgment of a whole people, from the solitary crime of an individual who acted from stern necessity.

Our voyage should not have exceeded six days, but head winds and calms prolonged it beyond all precedent. The weather was fine, and that's all I can praise. Our table was plentifully supplied, but of unfamiliar things that my coy appetite retreated from. I should have enjoyed a good roasted chicken occasionally, but a kind of remorse seized me when I reflected that but a couple of hours previously the poor confiding bird had been running around me. So I lived chiefly on rice, of an excellent quality and delightfully cooked.

Our passengers were quiet, pleasant people enough. There was a Mr. Stuart, an English gentleman, on his travels. Where don't the English go to? from the line to the poles! They are scattered over the earth, seeing everything, usually railing at most things, and they go back to their own comfortable country to pronounce it the best in the world. Mr. S. was a well-bred man, intelligent, and highly educated, and of agreeable refined manners.

There were several Americans making their annual pilgrimage to Cuba, where they spend their winters engaged in commercial pursuits, and return when pestilence warns them away. There was one fellow-passenger who attracted my attention by his solitary ways and silent habits; no one knew him, and he avoided acquaintance with all. He came to table, ate, spoke not, and retired. He spent hours gazing at the sea, and reading the rest of the day. He never talked with, and even never looked at any one.

The mysterious man in black made me very anxious to know who he could be. I conjectured, as all did at last, a thousand things; but the voyage finished and he departed, without giving token of where he came from or whither he was bound. I wonder what he was. We had one very rough gale. The inky black clouds and mutterings of thunder gave us threatening indications of what was to follow. No sense of security will ever subdue in me the anxious fears that will flit across my mind in moments like these. To go to bed on land with the wind rumbling down your chimney, your neighbors' shutters banging about, luckless tiles falling on the pavement with a crash, is startling enough; but how much more fearful

is a stormy night at sea; thick and angry-looking clouds flying hastily along, as if willing to wreak their malice upon your exposed head that no hospitable roof intervenes to protect! the thunder growls, lightning glares upon you; then the alarming preparations aboard, the hauling down of sails, the tying up of ropes, and everything else of an ambulatory nature; the howling of the wind like an evil spirit; then the cordage, the uneasy pitching of the vessel, and the dashing of the waters you can no longer see—all these make the getting up of a sea-tempest at night positively frightful. Then just when you are all tremulous expectation, waiting the onset of the furious elements, a brief request is made you to go to bed; in other words, to get out of the way.

With what reluctance and sinking of the heart I have complied with a demand useless to resist, it were impossible to describe. And what horror, too, to lie rolling in the narrow, uncomfortable bed, your ears dinned with appalling noises resembling the screechings of hideous fiends making darkness more terrible, a prey to the liveliest fears, and to every possible imagining! On this night, I shrunk into the low, dark, confined cabin assigned to us for our quarters; a sympathizing soul offered us his dormitory, and it would certainly have been far preferable, for our situation was distant and removed. No friendly voice to cheer, no hand to succor was nigh; but, to my astonishment, K—— refused this kindly offer before I could reply.

This was done in a mere braggadocia spirit; she saw I was frightened, and though she was doubtless more so, the occasion was too tempting for her not to assume a courage nowise natural, and attempt to shame me into a mortifying inferiority of my weakness, and her giant strength of mind. I remonstrated and entreated in vain, she only grew more perverse and laughed at my childishness. I resolved to punish her, should the occasion arise, and follow her through the men's cabin, who were generally retiring, and found our difficult way across the prostrate bodies of several who were compelled to pick the softest places along the main cabin floor, there being no other room for them, and at last we arrived at our solitary resting-place. We literally tumbled into our berths, but sleep or rest of any kind was quite out of the question ; it required constant and painful exertion not to be *thrown* violently out of bed. We were in the stern part of the vessel, and the pitching exceeded description or long endurance.

In five minutes I lost all identity, and had no idea whether we were above or below ; the darkness and roaring of the sea against the thin planks that shut me in from its fury, quite deafened me. At this conjuncture, as I expected, K——'s tremulous voice reached me. I could not hear what she said, but I guessed its import. I gave myself no concern about it, and was comforted in the midst of all by the agony of fear I knew she must be in. It was downright luxury after so much suffering through her vain folly. She screamed to go back ; I said nothing but held fast with the utmost difficulty. As usual, she took to flight ; of course I did not wish to be left alone, and followed her. Away went K—— in her night-clothes. I had not undressed.

Up stairs she flew, dashed open the door, knocking flat some unlucky creature happening to be near it, and took her affrighted course over the rolling bodies of the aforesaid passengers who were lying directly in her path ; not a few thought a bit of timber had fallen on them, and started up alarmed. I covered up her ignominious retreat with all the dignity the time allowed, but the captain nobly came to our rescue, and the same good creature who offered us a refuge before, now readily got up and resigned us possession of his deck-cabin. This time K—— accepted it with thanks boundless as her fears, and crept in without further parley.

I was willing to spare her the next day the humiliation of any recurrence to previous events. Thank Heaven, our voyage, that seemed destined never to end, began to approach its close ; we came in sight of the coast, and made a sort of a turn in and got between the main land and an island. We stopped off a place called Indian Key. What is locked up there that this key is meant to guard, I don't know. I saw little from the vessel— a shabby house or so, some green grass that looked very inviting, and all the rest looked perfect wilderness. The captain had his little boat lowered, and set to work to go ashore. He carried in his hand a small leather bag that seemed quite " full of nothing." I was wondering what he would bring back in it, and had the curiosity to inquire, when he told me conscious dignity that it was the United States mail committed to his charge, and that I was on board a *mail-packet* I now discovered for the first time. The winds have little care for government or correspondent, and it has been their special delight apparently to set both at defiance.

It is very good-natured, indeed, of the American government to send a vessel to this bleak and desolate part of the world, and I have great doubt if they are at all remunerated in postage, judging by the cadaverous condition of that leather-bag. The captain returned, bringing me a pretty *bouquet* of wild flowers—very gallant indeed ; and he told us some exciting stories of the terrible Indians, who are at war with the United States. It appears that some warrior, who has made himself formidable by his desperate courage and matchless cunning, has been taken, and it was hoped this would hasten to a close a contest that has endured for several years, with great loss to the whites who have had the combined horrors of a deadly climate, and savage ferocity to contend with.

My blood curdled in my veins as I listened to the recital of the revolting slaughter of the savages, who attack some defenceless settlement, lay it waste with fire and tomahawk, destroying indiscriminately their victims, without respect to age or sex. Their vengeance glutted, they fly back to their recesses in swamps, secure from pursuit or punishment. It is only by careful watching, and the most vigilant observation, that small parties of them are occasionally discovered, and then assailed. I lately heard an interesting account of an attempt to secure a ferocious band, who had secreted themselves on an island of an inland lake, so thickly strewn over with a deep and tangled vegetation, that the enterprise was deemed almost hopeless. The Americans set off in several boats, and proceeded with caution and silence to the designated spot.

The plan was to effect a landing unobserved, and fall vigorously upon the enemy ; but some too-eager youngster spoilt all by his rashness. Observing an Indian through the tall cane, he fired on him ; that gave the alarm, and shots were returned. The soldiers landed, and a running fight began ; but the Indians, with great adroitness, got off, leaving a few dead and wounded as the only spoil. All I hear of this strange race fills me with deep interest : in peace they are described to be a simple, virtuous, and dignified people ; in war, vindictive, relentless, and bloody : but they seem to regard the contest between them and the whites as one of extermination, and that alone can be alleged in extenuation of their atrocious butcheries. They cannot be considered cowardly for employing all the arts of cunning to inveigle them into ambush ; among civilized states stratagem is almost as often used, though it may be of a more elevated kind.

The Indian certainly meets death with a composure that neither philosophy nor religion can surpass. A tragic incident, related by an eyewitness, verifies this, if a thousand other proofs were wanting. There was a meeting of the chiefs of several tribes two or three years ago in the plains of the west to arrange a treaty with the government agents ; while sitting in the council, some of the young warriors amused themselves wrestling, when, in a moment of passion, one stabbed the other.

The unhappy murderer recovered his consciousness to feel he had committed a crime punishable with death, by the laws of his tribe. He went into the tent where the sages were sitting in calm deliberation. " Fathers," he said, " I have forfeited my life." He simply recounted the sad event, and added, " I am prepared instantly to meet my fate." He then stalked out, walked to a neighboring tree, and placing his back against it, he awaited the stroke. Two gray-headed men advanced, and without uttering a word, stabbed him to the heart. " I kept my eyes steadily on his face," said my informant, " and he never moved a muscle, and fell dead without a groan." This may be savage callousness, but it is affecting and imposing nevertheless.

As we sailed along the coast close in, the Indian watch-fires were pointed out to me, and we all speculated on our various fates should a storm arise, and wreck us upon this dangerous shore. It was jocularly supposed that I would be spared the horrors of the stake, if I once got the castanets on my fingers and danced the cachuca to the red sklns. That would, in truth, have been dancing *for my own benefit ;* and I promised in such an emergency to use my best influence to procure safety for all my fellow-passengers, if I was compelled to enter into an *engagement* on the spot.

After a night disfigured with unpleasant dreams, in which I imagined I was roasted and eaten with great relish by grinning savages, I got up sound and whole, to my great comfort, and looked out upon a day serenely beautiful, and whose temperature, for a January day, was soft and very warm, making heavy clothes uncomfortable, and protection from the too ardent sun of the tropics most desirable.

We were in sight of land, and the sea was so transparently clear that my eye could pierce its blue depths to the bottom several fathoms deep. I was in great spirits, and I chatted and read alternately. I got hold of an English book on the stage, by Alfred Bunn, Esq., a very clever and amusing work, rather slight in material, but well and sprightlily executed. Many characters portrayed are interesting, and the vicissitudes of management are fully shadowed forth. Even Mr. Bunn's prominent traits, fitting him so well for the task—great intelligence, energy and tact—effect little more than to involve him in loss and difficulty, when others would be entirely dismayed; but he manages, I don't know how, to get out safe again.

It was expected on board to-day that we should reach Havana to-morrow. What glorious news! How delighted I shall be to skip over solid ground again! Blow steady ye winds!—roll smoothly ye treacherous waves! Under these favorable circumstances we went into dinner, and the last chicken was eaten with the greater relish that it was the last; we were unusually gay, and I thought I saw some relaxation of the immoveable features of the silent man in black, but of that I will not be sure. I was just putting a spoonful of rice to my expecting mouth, when I experienced what I cannot exactly describe, but I felt sensibly the vessel had touched the ground or a rock. I dropped my spoon, and looked at the captain, who turned red, and got quietly but instantly up, and stole out on deck.

Bump, bump went the schooner, till all became aware of the accident; and certainly I never beheld a more sudden and complete change of expression from gay to grave, from lively to anything but serene. Some of the men were so alarmed that I grew more so. I had been told that this navigation was most dangerous, that the coast was lined with wrecks the whole year round, and that the route we were taking was perilous in the extreme—none, but one very familiar with its rocks, should venture it.

All the horrors of shipwreck rose up before my startled imagination, and the mischances of yesterday frowned closely upon us to-day; for if we escaped from drowning, we might fall into the hands of the Indians. So when I reflected terror began to seize me; but, thank Heaven! we escaped from the threatened calamity; for the captain, altering our course, the vessel got in deeper water, and we went smoothly enough again, but the incident quite damped all our spirits.

Next morning I was called up in great haste by K——, who was ready to jump overboard with delight to see a small town we were approaching, called Key West. I followed her, and certainly the sight was cheering and beautiful. A number of small white buildings lay scattered about in pretty groups—that was nothing unusual; but then the magnificent background—the splendid Oriental trees that greeted my enchanted sight, for the first time in my life! There they stood, the classic palm, the fruit laden cocoa, in their native soil; glistening in the bright rays of their own tropical sun, gaily waving their graceful heads in the morning air. I rubbed my eyes and gazed again, to be sure it was not a mere scene at the Opera House I was regarding, for there only had I ever seen any thing at all like this, and all my Eastern knowledge and associations spring from thence—but no, this was no trick of the sceneshifter—no stage display of painted pasteboard and counterfeit canvass—it was Nature herself—bright, beautiful, genuine Nature. Oh! what a lovely panorama spread itself before me! How my eyes strained themself to take in every object, and how my soul dilated and filled with joy, till tears of delight gave relief to my enchained feelings! This moment I shall never forget; it was one of those fairy sights that the eye so seldom rests on in this world, and it alone repaid me for all I had lost and left behind me. What enhanced, perhaps, the effect of this scene, was the contrast so fresh in my mind of the sharp cold and snows of the north.

Our handy little vessel drew up along the shore, and while they were rolling out some of those big, round barrels that had robbed us of so much room, K—— and I slipped off for a walk. We strolled about quite at our ease, exchanging the liveliest remarks, and staring at the cocoas, till one falling had nearly broken my luckless head. Enthusiastic as I was, I kept much greater distance ; and how pleasant it was to walk on earth again, to behold its brilliant vegetation, and breathe its fragrant odors. Unaccustomed to exercise, I returned quite tired ; imagine my surprise when, a few minutes afterwards, I was politely informed that the inhabitants were fully aware of my arrival, and that several of the richest planters had clubbed together, and were ready with any sum I might choose to demand, if I would only give them a dance—that suitable arrangement could be made in a few minutes in a large room—and that the vessel would be delayed awhile for that purpose.

I was not more astonished than flattered, for little did I dream of ever having been heard of in that distant and secluded spot. Expressing my kind acknowledgments, I declined ; when thinking, perhaps, I doubted their alacrity to pay the preposterous sum of one thousand dollars, which was offered to me, they proposed security, but to their great chagrin and disappointment, I persisted in my refusal, which I almost regretted, as their curiosity was really excited.

We set sail for the Havana, and passed several vessels as we left the quay that had lately been cast on this treacherous coast, and were now refitting. We had a fine fair breeze, and our little bark made good use use of it. We bounded along joyously. I was

struck, at night, with the crystal brightness of the skies, characteristic of those southern climes ; the heavens were studded with myriads of lustrous orbs I had never seen before. I had made friends with a sparkling trio as we came along the sea, and I now gazed on them with a familiarity founded on a two weeks' acquaintance ; how they twinkled and flashed when I looked at them, and I was glad to think I should see them again. I promised to make them the confidants of all my secret impressions of what I was going to see in this new land over which they were shining, and often afterwards I communed with them in moments when earth and its objects were far from my thoughts.   *   *

A more sunny smiling day than the 14th of January, 1842, never lit up this blessed world. I had risen early, full of longing and expectation. We were in sight of land at seven A. M., and we neared it rapidly. At nine I could easily distinguish objects, and the first one I could clearly discern interested me greatly ; it was a noble fortress commanding the entrance to the harbor, and called the Moro Castle. It had a yellow, mellow tint, that belongs to this delicious clime, and its rocky foundations had a look so firm and strong, as though they laughed to scorn the impotent waves dashing against its base.

There were several picturesquely dressed people sitting at various parts fishing as we swept by, which gave it an additional pleasing effect, and our vessel turned sharply round it, and with such dexterous quickness as though it remembered its well-known course, and what a sight broke upon me with all the suddenness of magic ! How magnificent and how indescribable ! I stood transfixed in wonder and delight. Before me lay the harbor, beautiful in shape, and its fine quays thickly lined with hundreds of vessels of all nations. Beyond it rose a green hill, adorned with many pleasing objects ; on the right stood the city, and several noble buildings instantly were presented to my eye; to the left ran a line of fortresses along a gentle elevation, covered with a verdant sward.

Great masses of idle people were standing contemplating our arrival, the vessels teeming with negroes oddly attired, who were at work rollng cargoes in and out, and accompanying their labor with a lively chaunt, both musical and strange. I stood entranced, utterly absorbed, turning only from one point to another of this novel and stirring picture, so full of objects, colors, and beauty, and glowing in a resplendent sunshine. Who that ever enter.ed the harbor of Havana on a fine day, for the first time, can forget either that glorious sight or the emotions it awakened? My impressions, I feel, are indelible.

As the vessel came to we were surrounded instantly with small boats of all sizes, with awnings over the sterns, a necessary protection from the rays of the sun, full of *commissionaires*, active in their offers of service. I had been recommended to a well-known hotel, called West's, and that person, a tall, stout man, with a sharp, knowing look, now advanced, saying he had reserved apartments, &c., and requested our passports that he might get a " permit to land." Soldiers came on board to prevent any one leaving without this required certificate, which I have heard occasions great delay and much expense. In half an hour, however, we got on shore near the Custom House. I looked in as I passed, and was vastly amused with the noisy scene of confusion it presented; filled chiefly with negroes most grotesquely costumed, and capering about among the boxes and bales like so many full grown baboons: but the din, the uproar, singing and yelling, beggared description, and made retreat soon necessary.

I was conducted to a *volante*, provided for our transit to the hotel; and was ever seen such a vehicle before? the oddest, drollest thing imaginable! What a sensation in would make in the Champs Elysées. I will send you a picture of one, Mina, for you can never realise it by any description of mine. It is something like a London gentleman's cabriolet, but hanging very low; and then such wheels, more than six feet in height, and the shafts in proportion. The horse, or mule more frequently, is harnessed almost at the end of them, so that the poor animal turns round a corner without your dreaming he is attached to anything, but directly comes in sight the ponderous *volante*. They contain two places, and are driven by a black, dressed as a *postillon*, with black gaiters, to match his face I suppose, instead of boots, called a *calasero*.

We got in and started under the auspices of Mr. West, and after several turnings through narrow streets, but clean and pretty, we arrived at our destination. We entered a high *porte cochère*, reminding me of the Parisian entrances, and, ascending a fine broad staircase, were ushered into the "apartment." This was the first shock I experienced, and it was a strong one, I assure you; quite a galvanic battery. The saloon, so called, was low and unpapered; there was a tile floor, scantily furnished with flimsy materials; with one window, and that *decorated* with iron bars, giving a very cage-like aspect to the place; and more than all, it was quite dark, by reason of the shadow of a house erected opposite.

The bedroom I reached by crossing a sort of viaduct, and found it small and uncomfortable; after the spacious and elegant hotels in the United States, I found such lodgings doubly offensive. I intimated pretty plainly, and I thought with reason, that I would prefer something better than that; but my host, though anxious to oblige, had nothing else. I found his house, large and fine in some respects, not adapted for an hotel. On the first floor we were lodged, but *à l'entresol*.

There was a showy saloon, intended for the common rendezvous of all the " boarders;" but there were no such things as sitting-rooms and bed-rooms adjoining; there were many of the latter, but all detached and unconnected. I found there was no other arrangement that would afford me the necessary privacy I required, and therefore with all the resignation I could summon, gave myself up to my dismal abode, hoping sooner or later, for relief.

As a matter of favor, we had our meals served in our saloon, for the custom is to meet at *table d'hôte*, which I declined, of course, for being regarded as a sort of lion or lioness, I did not care to be watched while *feeding*. I learned this occasioned a good deal of disappointment, as several curious persons, not living at the hotel, had secured places at the table to get a look at the " new arrival." Let these gastronomic enthusiasts come to the theatre and welcome. We despatched Charles, our zealous factotum, whose ruddy English face glowed again 'neath this tropical sun, to the Custom House for our baggage.

My *costumes de théâtre* were passed, and but few duties imposed. Great civility and attention were shown; but poor Charles compromised himself for the first time. Distracted as he was with the quantity and variety of our luggage, he was forced to put down a small straw basket he carried in his hand, containing several valuables. He selected a quiet, out of the way corner, and then returned to his active duties of opening and shutting boxes, bags, &c.

This accomplished, he went for his secreted basket; but, lo! it was gone —nowhere to be found, and no one had seen or touched it. His suspicions fell, of course, on the negroes attached to the establishment, for their active propensities at self-appropriation are undeniable and proverbial. Inquiry was useless, for among forty of them it was impossible to discover the rogue. It could have been none but one of these " officials," since all other persons are excluded from the sacred precincts beyond the Custom House gate. Charles came home with a

rueful face to announce his misfortune, which threw poor K—— into tears, for it happened, unfortunately, that a miniature of her deceased mother, the only one painted, was in the ill-fated basket, and she wept bitterly over this unexpected loss. My keys and some trinkets of value were also put there in the haste of the morning; but I forgot my loss in the more distressing one of K——'s.

An advertisement and handbill were published offering a considerable reward for the restoration of the miniature, but no tidings were ever heard of it. This was as yet the heaviest loss, and gave me a bad impression of negro habits. Had Charles been left to his own administration of justice, indignant as he was, he would very likely have wreaked his vengeance on the whole gang of woolly-headed rogues. To relieve his spirits and exercise his sharpened zeal, I gave him a secret and important commission to perform. My then quarters were insupportably gloomy, those hideous iron bars gave me the sensation of being in a dungeon, and as escape was not impossible, happily, in my case, I determined to make inquiry about another hotel which I had heard of, called by the hospitable title of the " Mansion House." As I did not wish Mr. West should know of my uneasiness, since his endeavors were constant to make me comfortable, it was necessary to employ a confidential person. Charles was, therefore, my emissary, and he could take no one with him to find the place, as it was a strictly secret affair. Off he started, not knowing a word of the language, nor a street, nor a person to help him in his discovery. By way of beginning, he got, when a little distance off, into a *volante*, and his adventures began. They were comical enough. He got out here and there, inquired in this shop and that, and finding his English of little service, tried pantomime.

At last he and his *calasero* fell out, and insisting with English doggedness on going his way, he got out, telling the blacky " to follow him ;" but as the latter could not comprehend him, he stood still, and Charles, after a smart walk, soon found himself worse off than ever, for he was minus the *volante*. Staring upward, as people will do when they don't know which way to go, he saw, looking him right in the face, the longed for and oft repeated words " Masion House." He made examination of the premises in question, and got safely home ; his report was very favorable, and I shall remove with every possible expedition. Adieu.

LETTER XX.

The Theatrical Autocrat, Don Marti—His History—Terms of Perfomance—A New Negotiator—The Theatre—Mademoiselle Borghese—Belisarius—The People of Havana—Their Houses and Balconies—Engagement at a Thousand Dollars a Night—Drilling the Supernumeraries—Spanish Pride—The Tacon Theatre—La Sylphide—Brilliant Success.

Havana, January, 1842.

My dear Henrietta—I know the deep and abiding interest you take in me, and I believe, notwithstanding our late misunderstanding, you have derived the heartiest pleasure on hearing of the good fortune which has attended me, and I hope you will not become indifferent to what will befall me hereafter. My travellings would lose half their attraction if you were no longer entertained by them. Here am I, your naughty Fanny, in Havana. I descended upon it suddenly, without any preparation, trusting, like Napoleon on his return from Elba, to the prestige of previous successes, and counting, also, on the natural curiosity excited, and the reputed taste of this people for the arts. Without making any contract, or receiving any propositions, I threw myself, unannounced, into the midst of the astonished natives, and left them to speculate upon my hardihood and future inventions. I sent no notice of my arrival to the sole manager of the theatres, Don Francesco Marti, nor meant to have delivered a single letter, but policy forced me o do so at an early moment. You hall hear how.

The day after my landing, and while anxious to know the result of my irregular proceeding, a message was brought in to the effect that Don Marti, the autocrat of all the theatres, would like to see me. " Faites l'entrée," I said, and immediately there came in the oddest-looking creature imaginable. Neither tall nor thin exactly ; loose white trowsers dangling on his legs, with an ill-shapen black coat thrown over his shoulders ; white cravat, and a great pin stuck in his shirt ; his hair was tossed over on one side, and a woman's side-comb secured it ; the face was colorless and wrinkled, and expressed great cunning. This apparition, on seeing me, clumsily raised its arms and cried out in a cracked voice, " Voilà la famosa !" and stared at me in right good earnest. He then announced himself and his business. He would like to make an engagement with me, but there were fifty difficulties, almost insurmountable, in the way.

I knew nothing of my man, and was therefore guarded. He talked a droll mixture of French and Spanish, which made me laugh in spite of myself. He said he would like to engage me for five or six nights, but then the difficulty to get those nights. He had his Spanish company performing at one theatre, his Italian company at another, and he could not think of disturbing their *funcion*, as he styled their representations. After a great deal of calculation and writing down about nights, he came to the point, and wanted to know my terms. I discovered immediately in Don Marti over-acuteness and great closeness; he had tried to frighten me with the uncertainty of my appearing at all, and was bent on getting me cheap; so I thought I would astonish him at once; and with great demureness I stated that I would accept 1000 dollars per night, a benefit for myself, a half benefit for my *maitre de ballet*, and some allowance for expenses of the three artistes I brought with me.

Don Marti, upon hearing this, looked at me to see if I was in earnest, then drew a long breath, put on his hat that he fitted tightly, and without saying a word, took his departure. I laughed heartily at his flight, and set to work to unpack, notwithstanding the doubtful state of things. I may as well tell you what I have since heard of this nondescript, who exercises undisputed sway over his managerial dominions in Havana. He is of Spain, and a Catalan, a large class here, remarkable for their unscrupulous cunning. Don Marti began his eventful career in this country, in the plain calling of a fisherman; and though he has since become a fisher of prima donnas and danseuses, he still sticks to his old trade. There is a story of his having betrayed to the government a ferocious pirate, who was the terror of this coast, and of his getting a large sum for it. The calumniators of the enterprising Don say that he was the friend of the pirate, and an assistant in his unprincipled work; but there is no sort of proof of this. The business flourished under his vigilance and industry; his one boat soon grew to a small fleet; and he then set to work to build

a fish-market, a neat but unpretending affair, that yields him a large revenue.

Just at this time the then captain-general, Taçon, offered to any contractor who would undertake building another theatre of grander dimensions than the existing one, materials for that purpose, and other important facilities. No one coming forward, our hero of the fish-market, all scaly as he was, presented himself, not from any refined sympathy for the arts, but never loth to drive a good bargain, whether selling a pirate, a basket of fish, or constructing a theatre. He agreed to the governor's proposals; but, first cautiously got twenty noblemen and gentlemen of Havana to buy a box in the new house for 1000 dollars each, by securing their custom and additional aid, he reserving the privilege to buy them in. In due time the edifice was erected, and dignified with the title of Taçon Theatre, and it is certainly one of the most splendid temples of art in existence; but of that another time.

Mr. West is a caterer of very nice dinners, though he complains greatly of the market, that it is badly supplied, and very dear; the *cuisine* is quite French, the wines also. The latter are largely imported direct from France, and are to be had of all qualities and at fair prices. We sat sipping our coffee when Don Marti came in, with an air of familiarity quite habitual to him. He got up a bad imitation of an apology, in alluding to his retreat of the morning, and began bargaining again. He was always making very stupid mistakes of one kind or another, but invariably in his own favor They served him but little, however, as I maintained but one position, fighting with him over what he declared an impassable barrier of 1000 dollars per night. When he found me immovable, he took his hat and ran away again, dropping something about his interpreter and coming back directly; and so he did in about an hour. He came this time supported with a very substantial prop, whom he introduced as his interpreter, Don Vellerino, a very stout man of under size, finely-formed head, and large, dark features. His manners were rather deferential, and not so ungraceful as his employer. He sat down with great gravity, spread a yellow silk handkerchief across his knees, and then said in very fair French that he came to explain Don Marti's meaning. We all began again.

Terms were re-stated, and we got no farther than before. Don Vellerino was plausible and ingenious, and he endeavored to accomplish by crafty manœuvring what his principal had failed to affect by coarser means. But I foiled them both, and kept my position; resisted the bold charges of Marti, and the insidious attacks of his man. They left me in despair, and nothing was settled. I went first to the Italian Opera given in the Teatro Principal, the oldest of the two theatres in Havana.

There is a third building devoted to dramatic purposes by an amateur company, but small and ill-constructed. But the Teatro Principal and Tacon are first-class edifices, and worthy especial notice. The former stands within the walls of the town, near the top of the harbor, and is well and conveniently situated. It has small pretentions to architectural beauty of any kind, and perfectly plain in style, and without ornament. The entrance is by two small doors under an archway, which open into a narrow corrider, with stairs to the right and left leading to the boxes. There is a ground-tier, also, enclosing the pit of very good size, divided in rows of seats, each one covered with red morocco, with arms and back, and numbered. Nothing can be more convenient and comfortable. These places are called lunettas, and are let at moderate prices for the night or for the season. So are the boxes, except those belonging permanently to several great families. In all, there are four tiers of boxes. The house is lofty, well-proportioned, and neatly decorated; the stage of ordinary size, and the scenery good; the orchestra strong, upwards of thirty performers in number, and of all colors, white, black, and yellow—a bit of mosaic harmoniously composed. Their performances are generally correct and effective.

Don Marti and his man are in the ascendant here. He got possession of this theatre with his usual good luck. It was managed previously by a volunteer commission of noblemen and gentlemen, who contracted for artistes, purchased scenery and wardrobes, and then began their operatic experiment. That went through the natural vicissitudes of so ill-judged an enterprise; the noble directors, occupied for the most part with the artistes, paid no attention to business, till loss, difficulties, and general confusion ensued, and they were disposed to get rid of it on any terms. Don Marti presented himself, and got the artistes and the addenda at a bargain, and the commission cheerfully shook off the cares and troubles of management.

The company now here is very good, including several artistes of very superior merit. The opera on this occasion was the well-known *Norma*, and I greeted it as an old friend. The impetuous priestess was sustained by a fair countrywoman of mine, Mlle. Ober—pleasing in person, with dark, expressive features. Her voice was agreeable, of good compass, sweet and flexible. She had cultivated it with considerable care, and sang correctly. Her chief fault lay in an excess of action, and a vehement expression of the passions, that greatly marred the effect. But she has soul and sentiment, the sure and only foundation of excellence; and many touches of her passionate acting went right to the heart.

She shared the honors of the evening with Mlle. Borghese, lately of the Opéra Comique, Paris, where I recollect applauding her in a very cleverly executed *rôle* in *La Fille du Régiment*, brought out for her *début*. She is a very sprightly and attractive singer, with a round and graceful person, expressive eyes, and glossy black hair. Her voice is naturally clear and musical, and well managed. I have seen her since in a more favorable part, well suited to her powers, the affectionate, devoted daughter of Belisarius; and I was greatly delighted with her singing and acting, the one neat and expressive, the latter finely shadowed and really touching.

Belisarius was performed by Salvatore, in whom I recognised at once a consummate artist; and his reputation is quite European. He came to the Havanna, hoping to find relief in its mild climate for his impaired health. His person is admirably adapted to the stage; tall, and perfectly formed, his fine eyes sparkle with intelligence, and his voice, a splendid organ, charms the ear with its rich, sonorous tones. He sung and played Belisarius to perfection. His indignant horror of his wife's treachery in the first act was admirably portrayed; but the succeeding scene, when he totters in blind and broken-hearted, quite overcame me. The despair, so appalling, expressed in the lower tones of his powerful voice, chilled the blood, and the heart gave way to the impassioned tenderness he threw into the recognition of his faithful child; singing the while with a true pathos and taste that drew tears of sympathy and admiration. Salvatore is a master of his noble art, possessing that finish and refinement which distinguish the great artist from his clumsy imitator.

While the curtain's down, *ma chère* Henrietta, you will pardon my looking round at the new faces about me. What a contrast to the fair complexions I have just left behind me! Here is every shade of brown, but set off with such fine dark eyes, glowing and flashing, that one is half afraid to look at them. Black hair and eyebrows finish the portrait, that is decidedly one of southern growth. I feel timid in giving first impressions where unfavorable; but I found the toilette of the ladies generally bad. It was mostly French; but their dresses were ill-made, though of the richest material, and had an ugly effect. I observed they wore no stays, and this gave a very sack-like appearance to their bodies, tied round, as they were, with a string. The Havana ladies are full to stoutness, falling, indeed, under the suspicion of fatness, which comes of their taking so little exercise—a sacrifice they willingly make to preserve the beauty of their small feet, most ludicrous disproportioned to the superstructure above. Their hands are pretty, and in public are most actively occupied with their fans, which they open and shut with a coquetry quite seductive. It is odd so much grace can be displayed in a thing so light. It is customary here for the men to visit between the acts, and I was honored by a call from Don Antonio Escovedo, to whom I brought letters, a person of high position and great influence, very stately in his manners, and grave as any Castilian is expected to be. He manifested a very flattering interest in my affairs, gave me a bad character of the indomitable Don Marti, advised me to insist on my demands, and rather to increase than abate them. He was certain to be fully remunerated.

This was consoling; and I settled into a deep, quiet determination that I would stand or fall where I was, *vis-à-vis* Don Marti. I received a visit, also, from a distinguished American, the Hon. Mr. E——, who has filled various high posts at home and abroad. He predicted that my success here would not be unworthy the example set in the North. I hope so! On leaving the Opera, I had some inconvenient proof that I had become an object of curiosity, for a thick crowd lined the whole way to my *volante*, and I feared I never should reach it. I am more comfortably lodged than I was. My saloon is lofty and cheerful, its chief recommendations; for the floor is of tile, agreeable enough in this hot climate, and very scanty of furniture. The house is large, and has seen better days, doubtless. Like all the fine mansions in Havana, it has a court-yard in the centre, and a wide corridor or gallery running round it, on a level with the first-floor. In this more airy situation the families spend the greater part of their time, breakfasting and dining here in preference to be enclosed within walls. These galleries are usually furnished with chairs and sofas, and are protected, too, from the sun, whose ardent embrace is rather shunned than courted by curtains of canvass.

There is one appendage to their houses I like above all others, the dear, delightful balconies that grace them nearly all, of every size, shape, and material. Nothing I love better than to saunter and loll up and down them, regarding the grave-looking houses above and below, and the many unfamiliar and droll objects in the streets. Mules laden with green corn, and belabored by little black boys, with a strong family resemblance to the monkey, yelling and shouting to the grave mule, who whisks his tail with Spanish superciliousness. And then those comical *volantes* I could look at for ever. With what deliberate caution they approach a corner! How nearly the practised *calasero* measures his space for shafts and wheels! And once clear, what a cracking of whips! Away he goes! The streets I like greatly. They are not paved, but hard and smooth, and carefully watered; very straight and narrow to exclude the sun. Many have awnings extended across, throwing a soft and gentle shade over them. The shops seem well supplied with foreign goods, French and English; but I have not been in them yet. I spy Don Marti and his man coming along the street. They look from their quiet manners—very unusual with them—as if their minds were made up. As the please! I found the clever Don had been actively at work to get up some party feeling against me. But I defeated his manœuvring by sending round my letters, which were quickly and kindly responded to. He begins to waver, I think. * * As I suspected, a decision has been demanded from Marti. He got no rest; clamors and questions on every side. The raving and remonstrating was repeated, till, at last, the all-potential voice of the captain-general was heard above the din; and Marti has submitted with a bad grace to his doom, as he regards it. I have signed with him an engagement of ten nights at 1000 dollars per night, and a benefit for myself, a half benefit for my *maître de ballet*, and 500 dollars for expenses of the two other artistes making my theatrical *suite*. He might as well have agreed at first, and he would have escaped the half-benefit for my ballet-master, Sylvain, whom you recollect I brought out from Paris with me. He has been, of course, highly useful, and very industrious and pains-taking. His conduct, in all respects, is quite unexceptionable. I am glad he is likely to be well compensated. The terms he agreed to in Paris were 150 dollars per week; but, as he was not bound beyond the first engagement at New York, he naturally sought to make hay while the sun shone. It beams in golden rays upon him here; for I give him 1000 dollars per month, and his half-benefit will produce him twice as much more. 3000 dollars for a month's drilling of his ballet recruits he is now beating up, is not bad pay. I have begun my practice again, and feared I should suffer badly after so long a vacation. But the warmth of the climate has been most favorable to me, and my limbs have recovered their pliancy and elasticity with far less labor than I apprehended. As I was skipping about the stage a day or two since with a buoyant vivacity that indicates my being pretty well *en train*, I heard to my surprise, an odd mixture of sounds, that was probably intended for a laugh, followed by a noisy clapping of hands. I looked about me, and beheld, in a dark corner of the theatre, the right worshipful Don Marti, who had been quietly inspecting, up to this moment, the *bargain* that was going to ruin him. I had not seen him smile since the first moment we met, and had no idea he *could* laugh; his rude admiration, therefore, was quite welcome; and as he sung out, quite lustily, "*Encora! encora!*" I went through my paces, and curveted and caracoled à l'Académie Royale, till I was out of breath. "*Eh, bien!* Don Marti. Buena! buena!*" cried he, in his own lingo, and, lighting his cigarito, he went puffing away, wearing a look of greater satisfaction than his uncomfortable face had yet assumed; not that he cared for or appreciated my caperings as a matter of art, but he began to think, perhaps, "it would draw."

It appears that M. Sylvain has desperate work to get up a *corps de ballet.* The town has been ransacked, and rewards offered; but such a thing as a *danseuse* of the lowest degree is not to be had. There are a few who practise Spanish dances, but they carry their heads far above ballet-work. Their noses rose haughtily at the bare mention of such degradation; and this, too, from the commonest people! Here's an awkward display of pride in rags—just the same sort of feeling that makes the Spanish beggar resist working, as an indignity, while he regards alms-taking or light-fingering as praiseworthy accomplishments. But I suspect our Havana dames of a natural apprehension, that from their unfitness they would risk becoming ridiculous. By dint of persuasion and authority, Don Marti has forced some of his female subordinates of the theatre into the ranks; but they are the most unpromising material that ballet-master ever worked upon. They are willing enough, poor things; but Nature never contemplated such a destiny for them, and has made them accordingly. Fat, ill-shapen, clumsy, and heavy, how can they ever be transformed into "sylphides?" Sylvain is persevering, but no conjurer; and such a miracle is not reserved for our days.

And, then, their color, so dark and swarthy, how can that be improved without scraping their faces?

Just conceive of a winged fairy of the Opera House, as radiantly white as pearl powder and gauze can make her, being personified by a plump mulatto, yellow as saffron, and as incapable of a feat of activity as a superannuated cow, and about as graceful. I am greatly distressed to see this fine ballet of *La Sylphide,* getting up for my *début,* marred in this lamentable way; yet I cannot help being entertained by this novel treat. I wonder how the people will take it? They must be good-natured, indeed, if not offended or annoyed by the sorry spectacle preparing. It may quite ruin me, for the ludicrous is a dreadful foe to contend with; and the waddling of these brown sprites may confound all my attempts at grace. *Nous verrons.* The prices have been inordinately raised; but quite half the places are already sold for the whole engagement.

This promises well, and Marti is likely to be a great gainer; for his Theatre Taçon, where I am to dance, is the largest, and he is the sole owner. It stands just outside the walls, and looks on the Paseo, or public promenade. It has a fine portico of stone stuccoed, but separated from the main building by a court-yard, into which carriages drive, letting down at the doors, three in number, opening on the ground tier. The interior is most striking; the size is very great, hardly surpassed by San Carlos or La Scala, and far more elegant in proportions and style. The tiers are five; but the first tier, instead of being panelled in, as usual, is adorned by a mahogany top bannister, with small gilt knobs. The effect is singularly pleasing and new.

The boxes are divided from each other, as in the Teatro Principal, by thin partitions of three feet in height, allowing full view and conversations between neighbors; and are provided with chairs, four or six, and varying proportionately in price. It is lighted by an immense chandelier hanging in the centre with oil-lamps; but they give a strong and sufficient light to all parts of the house, which, being painted chiefly in white, reflects it back again. I should observe, *en passant,* there are two places set apart for official dignitaries of the highest standing. The captain-general occupies in both theatres a capacious box, neatly fitted up, on the ground tier, near the stage; but just in front, in the principal tier, is a fine large one, more ostentatiously adorned, and occupied by a very important personage, the lieutenant-governor of the town, and the " president of the spectacle." In his latter office he exercises despotic sway. When the bell behind the scenes connected with his box once rings, the curtain must go up, and things must go on. If a song or a dance is encored, no repetition can follow without the consent of the bell, and which must be obeyed, whether disposed or not. I did not like this peremptory order of arrangement, though always willing to sacrifice myself to the public pleasure; yet moments arise when a woman is inclined to fall back upon her prerogative of doing what she likes, and I fear that my tongue and the bell will not always chime harmoniously. But I must be discreet in these parts, for the governors are formidable personages: they have an ugly power of suppressing disobedience, by putting refractory people where they may not like to go, in prison; and this, too, at the shortest notice.

To me, coming from countries where personal liberty is protected by the formalities of law, and where person and property are safe from arbitrary encroachment, I am not a little startled to find myself for the first time at the mercy of such summary proceedings. But, whatever inconvenience other luckless people may experience under such a *regime,* I have little to apprehend for myself, as I am decidedly popular already; and rebellious demonstrations will be treated, I trust, with great indulgence. I have a powerful patron in the Count de Penalver, an amiable and influential nobleman of great wealth, who acknowledged my letters to him with the fullest and kindest offers of service. The count is a Creole, and takes a lively interest in all that touches the credit or interest of his native country. He regards my coming here, as do the people generally, as highly complimentary—a sort of delegate from the grand centre of civilization, Paris, whose authority is reverentially acknowledged.

The Count de Penalver is a fair representative of his class, the native nobility. Easy and unaffected in manner, of engaging address, they conciliate at once the good-will of a stranger; their genuine good-breeding, courteousness, and refinement of taste, serve to complete their conquest over your good opinion. They have one quality in common, and to a depth and excess rarely met with—true, overflowing good nature. I had heard a great deal of the unsubstantial character of Spanish courtesy, that it was exceedingly liberal of offer but uncertain of performance. A true Castilian will invite you to the acceptance of his house, equipages, and purse; but always on the implied expectation that you refuse them. He would regard you as an unfledged barbarian were you guilelessly to take him at his word; but from the little I have seen of the noble Havaneroos, I find them earnest in their politeness, zealous in their efforts to oblige, and unceasing in kindness.

The count and his nephew called on me yesterday, and amused me greatly at the diverting stories he told of the excitement prevailing in the town to see me on the stage. The enthusiasm of their American neighbors has reached and infected them; their curiosity and impatience know no bounds, and they seem to have no definite idea in what the attraction consists. Opera dancing they know nothing about; and, as they are informformed that my style is totally differ ent to the languid measure of their national boleros, they are lost in conjecture. Not a few expect to see me scaling the chandelier, and alighting on the top row of boxes. I shall never, certainly, come up to such expectations. I begin to apprehend the recoiling effect of the curiosity that rises higher in every succeeding place I visit. It is impossible to keep pace with the exaggerated praises bestowed upon me, and sooner or later I shall come down, as all artificial greatness does.

I will not send off this letter till I can send you an account of my *debut*, which takes place to-morrow night. * * * * * It is over. The ordeal was trying, and for a while the result seemed uncertain ; but I have got good hold of them now, and the ground is firm under me. I was just setting out for the theatre on the eventful evening of my first appearance, when an elegant equipage, with outriders, drove up, to carry me there, with the compliments of the Count de P. This was highly gratifying, if not a novelty ; for at Berlin I never went to the palace but in a royal carriage : but then the king and queen had always been partial to me. Such an attention from a stranger was hardly to be expected. Crowds were pouring down to the theatre, round which stood a thick mass as I drove in. I felt a little trepidation, not so much for myself, as I had already gone through such stirring scenes, but for the adventurous " sylphides" of native growth, who were to unfold their wings for a first flight.

The curtain rising, discovered me on the stage. I was recognized by a few, who communicated the secret to the rest in the usual way, and the whole house broke into hearty applause. The crowd was immense, between 3000 and 4000, and the effect was indescribably fine. The men, as customary here, winter and summer, were all in white trowsers and dark coats ; the ladies in white. These light dresses were seen through the pretty rail around the boxes, and gave a bright, cheerful aspect to an audience I have never seen equalled. The bravos soon died away, and the most intense silence succeeded. The eyes had it their own way, and how they did stare.

There is little in the first act of *La Sylphide* to excite much fervor ; but I found them getting much too chilly for my taste. The appearance of the " sylphides " provoked, as I anticipated, great merriment ; and, truly, they were irresistible. Their dresses were exceedingly ill made ; their wreaths of the cheapest materials ; and, by way of abating the effect of their brown bosoms, Don Marti had encased them in bright yellow *chemisettes*. This was putting powder on the fire. Their arms and legs were left to take care of themselves. Just before they went on the stage, the ballet-master, Sylvain, determined, in a moment of desperation, to *whitewash them*, which he actually effected with a large brush and some white mixture. I leave the effect to your imagination. But the second act was to decide my fate, and theirs. I felt the public were not with me yet : they were cold, almost indifferent. This piqued me, and I decided on attacking them vigorously. The moment came, and my efforts were not unavailing. "*Mes pointes,*" astonished them, and the applause was vehement. I quitted the stage pretty well satisfied. It was now the time of the " sylphides." They began, amid the silent wonder of the house. For a while they observed order ; but some fatal evolutions threw them into confusion. Sylvain shouted at them, " Right !" " left !" from the side scenes ; but this only confounded them the more. They looked at each other in dismay ; the audience began to hiss, and away they went in a scamper right off the stage.

One luckless creature was too heavy and short-winded to keep up with the rest ; she got fairly distanced, or, perhaps, was not aware at first of the decampment of her companions. My eye fell upon her as she stood in the centre of this great stage. Horrified at finding herself quite alone, she set off on a brisk trot to the right; but then changed her mind, wheeled round, and broke into a wild gallop of her own composition. This was too much for the house; they fell into convulsions of laughter that I thought would never end.

I was heartily vexed, as fearing it would be disastrous to me; but who could retain gravity with such a grotesque event to overturn it? and I laughed along with the rest. It was impossible to bring the house back to sobriety; the sight of these yellow fairies at once infected them, and the ballet proceeded amid a badly suppressed titter. The "Cracovienne" succeeded, and, though warmly applauded, it did not produce its usual effect. I returned home quite chagrined, and would have, at that moment, gladly rescinded the contract, and not appeared again.

The ensuing day I received an early visit from Don Marti and his man, who were both greatly alarmed, and attributed the comparative failure of the previous night to my want of attraction, rather than to the unrehearsed effects that happened. He absurdly proposed a change of ballet; that would require a week's labor, and a change of dance; I calmed his apprehensions by my assurance that I would guarantee him against loss, but was determined to change nothing, and go on. He went away with a doleful and doubting face. The second performance came, and I had guarded against similar mischances by clipping the *corps de ballet* of some of the fattest and yellowest of its numbers, and thus reducing it to a smallness ludicrously in contrast with the vast size of the stage; but this was better than mere caricature putting illusion out of countenance. I determined to depend on myself alone. I felt no fear, and challenged the result. The house was filled to overflowing, less buzzing and eagerness; expectation more subdued, and attention more close and critical. This suited me exactly, and I did my best. The audience grew warm in the first act. I perceived they were moving; but the second act carried them clean away out to a sea of enthusiasm that dashed and roared till its mighty billows nearly frightened me.

The "Cracovienne" accomplished all the rest, and my triumph was complete. I was called out different times, and the stage was converted into a gay parterre of lovely flowers. As I passed Don Marti on leaving the theatre, who stood at the door all radiant in grins, I good-humoredly asked him if he would like to change the ballet now. "Non, non, Famosa jamais!" Yours truly.

THE END

The Chevalier Henry Wikoff.

Vanity Fair. From The New York Public Library Collection.

Edouart silhouette of Henry Wikoff, Philadelphia, 1843. Mr. and Mrs.
H. Gregory Gulick.

The Triumph of the "Satanic Press."
From The New York Public Library Collection.

Sad Tale of the Courtship of

CHEVALIER
SLYFOX-WIKOF

SHOWING HIS HEART-RENDING,

ASTOUNDING & MOST WONDERFUL LOVE ADVENTURES WITH

FANNY ELSSLER AND MISS GAMBOL.

SAD TALE OF THE COURTSHIP OF CHEVALIER SLYFOX-WIKOF, SHOWING HIS HEART-RENDING, ASTOUNDING & MOST WONDERFUL LOVE ADVENTURES WITH FANNY ELSSLER AND MISS GAMBOL

The magazine *Yankee-Notions* in March 1855 illustrated its cover with a cartoon of Horace Greeley, Wikoff and P. T. Barnum, quills in hand, busy at their respective memoirs, with the caption: "Triumph of the 'Satanic Press.'" The newspapers had reported garbled and melodramatic accounts of Henry Wikoff's tour de force with Miss Jane Gamble, and his memoir, *My Courtship and Its Consequences*, he hoped would vindicate his good name. But it was the scurrilous stories in the newspapers and Wikoff's earlier "courtship" with Fanny Elssler which inspired one of the earliest comic strips.

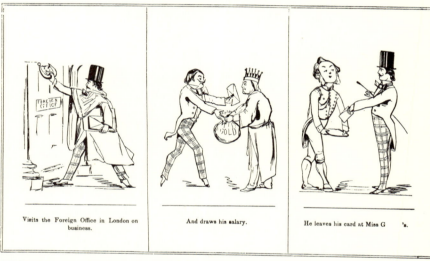

Visits the Foreign Office in London on business.

And draws his salary.

He leaves his card at Miss G——'s.

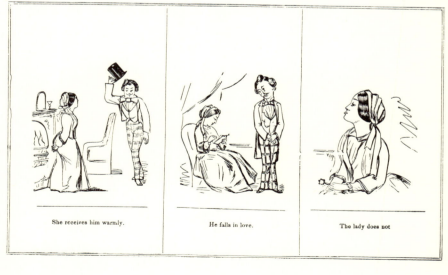

She receives him warmly.

He falls in love.

The lady does not

Thinks her income, united to his own, would soon be sufficient for all the exigencies of married life.

He meets her in the country and they enjoy themselves considerably.

Which induces him to write a proposal.

And delivers it.

The lady cannot make up her mind

So he throws himself at her feet.

And she throws cold water on his hopes.

A German friend consoles him.

And he is further encouraged by a Valentine from the lady.

And rushes off to see her.

She demands the return of her letters.

And attempts to burn them.

She has a bad dream of him.

Whilst he thinks of suicide.

The Duke of Wellington advises him not to do it.

Portrait of the Courier he feels uncomfortable about.

So he follows her to Switzerland.

Unhappy because he cannot find her

He nabs the nurse, however.

She advises him to continue the chase

He buys a trout to present to her.

Fraternises with the Monks of St. Bernard.

And surprises the Lady.

Gradually concluding to let her slide.

And bolts.

Another meeting. He proposes,—the Lady yields, and says " Go along, yes."

She determines to fly to Stamboul, but an apparition of the Plague scares her from it.

He scorns her cash.

She asks him to take care of her a week, whilst the Courier is gone.

Courier returns from the bosom of his family—rather high.

Wikof gets the sack once more.

Thinks better of it.

In despair.

He packs his trunk.

Mary, the nurse, superintending.

Sees her again in the garden. She confesses her love.

And names the day.

Count D'Orsay and.

Louis Napoleon congratulates him on his successful diplomacy.

A rival comes on the stage.

Bates declares he won't interfere.

Mrs Grote volunteers some advice to Miss G

Who brings Mary to tell him she cannot marry.

He bribes her courier.

And he luxuriates on the money.

He makes up his mind.

To take her prisoner.

When she writes another promise of marriage.

And to show her pains, breaks his panes with a poker.

And goes into hysterics.

They both indulge in hysterics.

She begs forgiveness.

Takes a walk by moonlight with him.

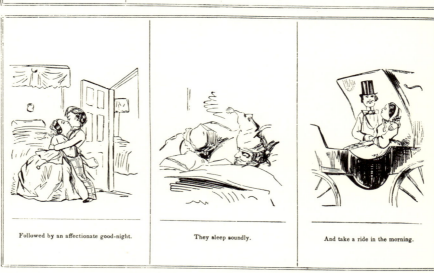

Followed by an affectionate good-night.

They sleep soundly.

And take a ride in the morning.

When he is gone, she goes to the British Consul.

The British Lion is aroused.

So is the Police.

He is defended by the majesty of the
Stars and Stripes.

It's no use, however.

And his enemies triumph.

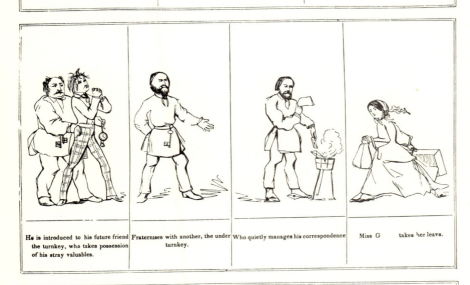

He is introduced to his future friend
the turnkey, who takes possession
of his stray valuables.

Fraternises with another, the under
turnkey.

Who quietly manages his correspondence

Miss G   takes her leave.

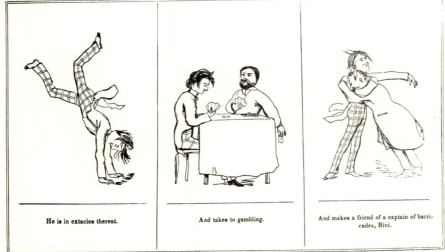

He is in extacies thereat.

And takes to gambling.

And makes a friend of a captain of barri-
cades, Bini.

Who initiates him into the mysteries of maecaroni.

And overcomes Roquino.

He learns Miss G—— returns to prosecute.

Quakaro endeavors to console him.

For the look of the thing, he goes to trial in a carriage.

And is placed face to face with Miss G

The Judges take their places.

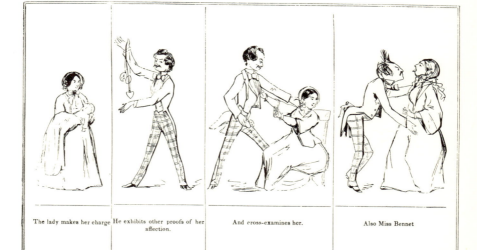

The lady makes her charge

He exhibits other proofs of her affection.

And cross-examines her.

Also Miss Bennet

And Mary the nurse.

As well as several landlords of hotels.

While Brown has a private conversation with the Judge.

Next the United States Consul is examined closely.

Lawyer E. Brown tries to bribe landlord.

The Public Prosecutor demands sentence to the galleys for fifteen years.

Miss G   calls him a liar.

The Judge jugs him for fifteen months.

And she goes off with Brown.

He sends application for a pardon.

The British Ambassador jumps in.

Miss G. visits the prison.

Just as Roquino takes revenge on Bini.

Who is acquitted.

Wikof makes the acquaintance of several
industrious fleas

And enjoys a numerous correspondence.

And the omelets of the Courier.

Who he allows to sleep under his bed.

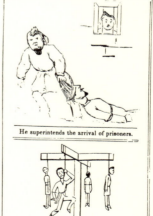

He superintends the arrival of prisoners.

Not to mention a few executions.

His culinary arrangements are disturbed by
the arrival of the Director of the Prison.

As a special favor, he is allowed out-door
exercise.

Miss G   offers him some money to
let the whole thing drop.   His indignant refusal

Makes the acquaintance of a gentlemanly
hangman.

And a remarkably aristocratic Frenchman.

The last day arrives.

And he regales his prison friends.

And leaves with a stiff upper
lip.

To enjoy a night's rest in a good bed.

Dreams Miss G   and Fanny Ellsler are one.

And of a morning visit he paid her.

To pay her a little money on account.

Which she received with thanks,

Expressed by a little fascinating ballet, in which he joins.

Also a little acrobatic entertainment

After which they refresh.

He concludes it would be no use to abduct her.

His dream continues, and he is once more proprietor of a Tea Store.

From which he is abducted by a widow.

Miss G____ releases him.

And he escapes with her in a Tea Chest.

Chased by Brown.

And finally caught.

And jammed into Brown's hat.

From which unpleasant situation he is awakened by his guardian angel.

The appearance of his nose next day.

He mends his stockings.

To prepare for an interview with Brown, who is defiant.

The Marquis Cavour throws all blame on the British Government.

Gets back to Paris and pleasure, and

To London, where he examines Miss G.'s defences

Under Secretary of State promises justice.

He determines to write his book.

Miss G   offers through American Consul to buy coppright for £10,000.

And admits to his landlady that if she had not loved him so much, she would not have gone so far.

Bates acts the Jesuit to the last.

Effect of the book on his nerves.

And on Miss G

On Brown's.

On Lord Palmerston.

On Mrs. Grote.

The effect of the publication of these Illustrations

IDEAL PORTRAITS OF THE CHEVALIER WIKOF.

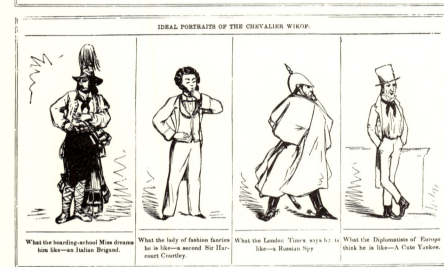

What the boarding-school Miss dreams him like—an Italian Brigand.

What the lady of fashion fancies he is like—a second Sir Harcourt Courtley.

What the London Times says he is like—a Russian Spy

What the Diplomatists of Europe think he is like—A Cute Yankee.

IDEAL PORTRAITS OF THE CHEVALIER WIKOF.

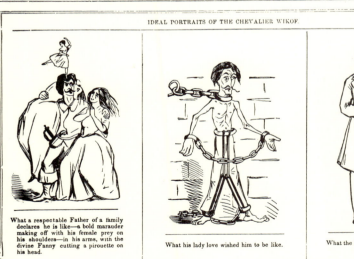

What a respectable Father of a family declares he is like—a bold marauder making off with his female prey on his shoulders—in his arms, with the divine Fanny cutting a pirouette on his head.

What his lady love wished him to be like.

What the Picayune knows the Chevalier to be like.